A VOICE
FROM INSIDE

First edition August 2021

Book design by Nuno Moreira, NMDESIGN.ORG

ISBN 9798522840051

A VOICE
FROM INSIDE

Notes on Religious Trauma
in a Captive Organization

GEOFFREY WALLIS

CONTENTS

Introduction: A Captive Organization 9

1. The PIMO Perspective 19

2. Chronicling Captivity: The Path Toward High Control 31

3. The Mechanics of Psychological Captivity 69

4. A Crisis of Conscience: Ethical Implications 93

5. An Introduction to Religious Trauma Syndrome (RTS) 123

6. A PIMO Faces Religious Trauma Syndrome 143

7. A Day in the Life of a PIMO 165

8. Transcending Ideological Dogma in the Broader Community 191

An Open Letter to the Governing Body 209

Author Bio 213

References 215

Introduction: A Captive Organization

"As I understand it, people who no longer want to be known as one of Jehovah's Witnesses, but who have been, must then disassociate; is that right?" says Angus Stewart, the Senior Counsel Assisting to the Australian Royal Commission into Institutional Responses to Child Sexual Abuse (Royal Commission, 2015).

Stewart looks briefly up at the oath-bound witness and then back at his notes in a non-confrontational gesture that belies the implication of his questioning. Across from him is a TV screen projecting a videoconference feed of Geoffrey Jackson, a member of the eight-man governing body of Jehovah's Witnesses responsible for the spiritual and organizational leadership of over 8.5 million Jehovah's Witnesses worldwide.

> Jackson: No, not necessarily. I meet many people in my travels that perhaps were Jehovah's Witnesses at one stage but then have decided no longer to be active. So, they haven't gone through a formal process.
>
> Stewart: Well, I have chosen my words deliberately, Mr. Jackson.
>
> Jackson: Okay.

Stewart repeats the question, challenging Jackson's

evasion.

> Stewart: If someone no longer wants to be known as one of Jehovah's Witnesses, they must then disassociate; is that right?

> Jackson: Again, please, if they want to take the action of doing that. But, of course, they have total freedom. If they don't want to apply to officially be removed as one of Jehovah's Witnesses, they can tell anyone they want that they are no longer a Jehovah's Witness.

The prosecutor then reads from the official policy of Jehovah's Witnesses regarding the procedure for discontinuing membership as one of Jehovah's Witnesses. The policy is clear: if a Jehovah's Witness (JW) decides that she no longer wants to be a member of the religion, she must disassociate herself and will be shunned from the community. Further, if she chooses not to formally disassociate but is later discovered to have violated the organization's strict code of conduct, she will be disfellowshipped. Disfellowshipping refers to the disciplinary policy within the JW community of formal excommunication from the religion. The policy also calls upon close friends and blood relatives to shun the disfellowshipped person.

Stewart again attempts to hold Jackson to the unambiguous policy of disassociation and disfellowshipping enforced by the influential preacher's organization.

> Stewart: So is it the case, then, that someone who

no longer wants to be recognized as or known as one of Jehovah's Witnesses must then disassociate?

Jackson: No, it doesn't say that they *must* do anything. If you read on, you will see there is a process. This gives the person the right to officially have an announcement made that they are no longer one of Jehovah's Witnesses. But, as I already said, if they decide they don't want to exercise that right, they don't automatically come under this provision.

Stewart: But then people who don't exercise that right are then (…) still subject to the rules and discipline of the organization, aren't they?

Jackson evades again.

Jackson: I would have to check on that, because personally that's not my field. But my understanding is, if a person has made it known by their actions in the community over a period of years that they are not a Witness, we would only hold any reports in abeyance until they decided they wanted to return.

Stewart: Mr. Jackson, I have to say that my understanding is if someone in that position is caught transgressing one of the rules, they would still be subject to the disciplinary proceedings, including possibly disfellowshipping; is that not right?

Jackson: That is a possibility, but in all fairness to

your question, I think there are circumstances, but I couldn't make a definitive comment on that.

The prosecutor goes on to present a hypothetical in which a JW who chooses not to formally disassociate and face shunning from his friends and family is caught by congregation elders in the act of celebrating Christmas or a birthday (customs considered by JWs to be part of false religion and offensive to God).

> Stewart: They would be found to be in transgression of the rules, would they not?

> Jackson: That is not my understanding. But again, as I said, it is not my field, that goes into policy with regard to those types of things, but from my personal experience, that's not the case.

> Stewart (indignantly): Mr. Jackson, you say it's not your field, but you are a member of the Governing Body which is responsible, as you have said, for the whole field, and you have been a member for 10 years, and all the committees are responsible to and accountable to the Governing Body.

> Jackson: That is correct.

At this point in the proceedings, Stewart is only barely able to conceal his frustration. Official policy is clear: every JW is subject to the rules of the organization under threat of judicial action. This includes prohibitions on premarital sex, the celebration of holidays, voting, and violating the policy of shunning by having unsanctioned association with ex-member family or friends.

> Stewart: Well, there's no middle road, is there? I mean, you are either a member and subject to the organization or are not—isn't it the case?

> Jackson: Yes, but I thought you were asking me about disassociation.

> Stewart: Well, I am, indeed. So if someone hasn't disassociated but has sought merely to become inactive or to fade [away from the organization], they are then still subject to the organization's discipline and rules?

> Jackson: If they acknowledge being one of Jehovah's Witnesses.

> Stewart: And if they do the contrary—which is to say they are not one of Jehovah's Witnesses—the effect of that is disassociation?

> Jackson: That's if they decide to go down that course.

> (...)

> Stewart: So someone who wants to leave the organization must choose, you accept, between freedom from the organization on the one hand and friends, family, and social network on the other?

Jackson refuses to concede.

> Jackson: I thought I made it quite clear that I don't agree with that supposition (…)

> Stewart: Mr. Jackson, the reality of the situation is that a person who has been baptized a Jehovah's Witness is thereafter either in the organization or out of it; is that not right?

> Jackson: I think perhaps you have got your facts a little wrong there.

> Stewart: I don't think that's correct, because you have accepted already, Mr. Jackson, that a person in the situation you have postulated of merely becoming inactive is still subject to the rules of the organization.

Jackson deflects. His tenacious refusal to admit, or perhaps even to comprehend, the implications of the group's coercive policy is confounding. Finally, Geoffrey Jackson unequivocally presents his stance on the point of contention.

> Jackson: I don't agree with the sweeping statement that they only have the two choices.

> Stewart: Well, it's right then, isn't it, because if they don't want to be subject to the discipline and rules of the organization, then they have to leave by actively disassociating; isn't that the truth?

Jackson: That's if they definitely don't want to be, yes.

Stewart is dogged; he does not let the point go. Quite rightly. His argument at the Australian Royal Commission's inquest into institutional responses to child sexual abuse was that when a victim of sexual assault at the hands of a fellow congregation member feels compelled to choose between avoiding congregation meetings or sacrificing their closest family and friends, they feel trapped. Victims may feel that they must continue attending congregation meetings, sitting in the same room with their abusers who have been deemed repentant by congregation elders, or otherwise face official excommunication and shunning.

The challenges of child sexual abuse in the JW community are complex indeed and worthy of a separate volume completely. Respectfully, I will not discuss this topic at length in this one. But as Stewart proceeds with his examination, he touches on a dilemma that sets the stage for *A Voice from Inside*. He continues:

> Stewart: Do you accept that putting people to that choice makes your organization in many respects a captive organization?

> Jackson: I do not accept that at all.

Stewart chose not to use the oft-repeated pejoratives for New Religious Movements (NRM) like Jehovah's Witnesses. Accusations of cultism are met not only by official personnel but also by rank-and-file JWs with organizationally prescribed and pre-rehearsed statements of defense. The use of "cult" in this courtroom setting may have triggered a canned defense from the Governing Body member who may have interpreted the prosecutor's scathing criticism as evidence of divine favor. (Indeed, as St. Paul the Apostle wrote, "all those desiring to live with godly devotion in association with Christ Jesus will also be persecuted" [2 Timothy 3:12; Watch Tower, 2013a]).

Like Stewart, I have also decided to avoid defamatory language in *A Voice from Inside*. I do not intend to argue that JWs are a cult. I will not accuse the group's leadership of brainwashing their followers. Instead, I will follow the custom of the academic and scientific communities who employ the terms New Religious Movement (NRM) and High Demand Religious Group (HDRG) when referring to JWs. These categorizations are accurate, maintain a level of respect for the beliefs of adherents, and afford individual members dignity. For the sake of clarity, I will use the term Jehovah's Witness (JW) to refer to individual members of the religion, and Watch Tower Society (WTS) to refer to the community that they make up.

In Chapter 3, "The Mechanics of Psychological Captivity," I will discuss at length the psychological principles associated with what psychiatrist and author Robert Jay Lifton calls ideological totalism. I cite heavily from Robert Jay Lifton's *Losing Reality: On Cults, Cultism, and the Mindset of Political and Religious Zealotry* to draw connections between aspects of JW life that coincide with Lifton's theory of thought reform; a theory he derived from his research into the Chinese Party's formalized indoctrination of Chinese citizens in communist principles. I will argue that ideological totalism aptly applies to the WTS community. However, as the title of Lifton's book suggests, many academics acknowledge the proximity of ideological totalism and cultism; a proximity that is at the root of emotion-laden accusations of culthood launched at JWs and WTS. Lifton explains his view of the relationship between the two sociopsychological concepts when he states: "I came to realize that ideological totalism and cult-like behavior not only blend with each other but tend to be part of a single entity (…) Totalism and cultile behavior are not separate identities but part of a common constellation" (Lifton, 2019).

However, to avoid unnecessary semantic controversy, I will focus my discussion on the expression Angus Stewart used at the Australian Royal Commission inquiry: captive organization. Because of my upbringing and active membership as one of JWs, the dialogue between Mr. Stewart and Geoffrey Jackson (made available on YouTube) was my first exposure to this unique expression. Stewart's use of "captive organization" was fresh and arresting, bypassing the well-oiled psychological defenses and the synaptic potentiation of my cultural theology.

Frankly, it set me back.

> Stewart: Well, there's no middle road, is there? I mean, you are either a member and subject to the organization or are not—isn't it the case?
>
> Jackson: Yes…

Stewart and Jackson finally agree. There is no middle road.

1. The PIMO Perspective

One cannot help but notice the strong bias in books about JWs. On the one hand, literature published by the Watch Tower Bible & Tract Society of Pennsylvania Inc. is published to support the organization's mission. Conversely, counter-cult literature and personal commentary from the ex-JW community are intensely critical, calling attention to a variety of grievances ranging from doctrinal inconsistencies and failed prophecies to child sex abuse cover-ups.

In his book *Jehovah's Witnesses: Continuity & Change*, George Chryssides alludes to this polarization when he refers to the "insider–outsider problem" of writing objectively about WTS and JWs. He raises the question: who can most accurately understand a religious group, particularly one, like Jehovah's Witnesses, that seems so enigmatic?

> Is it the insider, who is immersed in the tradition and practices it faithfully? Is it the critic, who does not have vested interests in defending the organization, and can see its faults as well as its attractions? Is it the academic, who endeavors to appraise a religious movement as objectively as possible, eliciting accurate information, but who may be aridly detached, lacking any kind of enthusiasm for either side? (Chryssides, 2016, p.12)

There is, however, a group that Chryssides does not mention above. It is the insider who, although fully immersed in the tradition and culture of JW life, practices it irreligiously, and has in a most intimate way reckoned with both the faults and attractions of the organization. Could it be this subset most fit to understand the culture and theology of WTS? Could it be the physically in, mentally out (PIMO) Jehovah's Witnesses?

In his well-researched and "aridly detached" (Chryssides, 2016, p.14) academic discussion of JWs, Chryssides modestly leaves the judgment of what is good and bad in the religion to his readers. While I too will attempt to discuss this religion with respect for the deeply held beliefs of its members and avoid the use of sarcasm or inflammatory vocabulary, I cannot avoid the confrontationality of the topic matter of *A Voice from Inside*. As explained in later chapters, the circumstances of the PIMO Jehovah's Witness necessitate an ability to balance personal grievances toward the religion with an awareness of the weighty ethical implications of an allegation of organizational captivity and Religious Trauma Syndrome (RTS) of disillusioned members.

That is not to say that there is not a healthy dose of criticism in this work. Chapter 4 presents an ethical consideration of certain aspects of WTS theology and policy that appear to relate to the experience of RTS. I also have included a call to action for WTS leadership and politically and socially influential readers, encouraging them to consider what must be done to protect the rights, freedoms, health, and safety of citizens who may be at risk in the organization.

This volume is mute on any potentially advantageous components of JW theology or cultural environment. An exhaustive commentary on the positive features of JW life is repeatedly provided by the organization itself (see JW.org for more information). In fairness then, and to moderate my criticality, I have narrowed my argument to the following thesis: It is my opinion that the combination of theology and policy within WTS creates an atmosphere of psychological and organizational captivity that causes the PIMO phenomenon and may result in the onset of Religious Trauma Syndrome (RTS) for some disillusioned members.

Physically In, Mentally Out

PIMO is an acronym for "physically in, mentally out" that came into usage within internet communities of disillusioned and ex-JWs. The term refers to a person who belongs to an HDRG but decides that the repercussions for leaving are too great, and therefore chooses to maintain membership despite no longer agreeing with the organization's religious tenets or mission. It is a hashtag really, used by card-carrying members of WTS, usually under an alias, within online communities of ex-members and other PIMOs.

PIMOs are from all walks of life and may exist at all tiers of the WTS hierarchy. They are teenagers who became formal members of the organization upon baptism in their preteen years. They are mothers who, in the religious zealotry of their past, raised their children to become baptized JWs. They are husbands and fathers who proliferated the religion's oppressive doctrines within their own families. They may have served the organization for decades as full-time ministers, overseers in local congregations, or as volunteers at WTS headquarters.

But they are disillusioned. And they are stuck.

Research regarding the traumatic consequences for members of HDRGs who chose to leave their organizations is increasing in recent years. A principle work in the discussion of this phenomenon comes from Dr. Marlene Winell, who coined the phrase "Religious Trauma Syndrome" (RTS) in 2011 and published a series of articles about the condition in the British Journal *Cognitive Behaviour Therapy Today*. Dr. Winell defines RTS as follows:

> RTS is a function of both the chronic abuses of harmful religion and the impact of severing one's connection with one's faith. It can be compared to a combination of Post Traumatic Stress Disorder (PTSD) *and* Complex PTSD (C-PTSD) (Winell, 2011)

After being severed from their religious community, RTS victims may benefit from support groups of fellow ex-members or in various other embracive communities. With much effort and the empathetic assistance of mental health professionals, many integrate successfully into the larger community and maintain a sustainable lifestyle. Understandably, the research regarding the effect of NRMs on individual mental health centers around the individuals who exit. Still, much work to raise awareness of effective treatments for such individuals remains to be done.

Some readers will be familiar with literature published by ex-JWs who go on to become outspoken activists against spiritual abuse. For these ambitious and extroverted types, writing a book or streaming a YouTube channel chronicling their spiritual journey and trauma recovery is an understandable expression of their newfound liberty. Indeed, their work provides an important perspective for outsiders and gives a voice to the suffering of so many.

However, it is the introverted and perhaps less outspoken personality types among WTS who often, despite disillusionment, make the difficult choice to stay. In some cases, these individuals may choose not to leave their social communities for purely pragmatic reasons; financial, employment, or housing considerations. Perhaps others don't make friends easily and live in significant fear of social connection outside of the religious community of their birth. They may desire to keep the intimacy of their close friendships from among JWs, and value the relationships that they have cultivated over the years. The point is that such soft-spoken empaths and Highly Sensitive Persons (Benham, 2006) are often the very ones who become PIMOs, the very ones who suffer the worst post-traumatic symptoms, and the very ones whose voices go unheard. While awareness grows as to the effects of RTS upon ex-members, the plight of the PIMO goes largely unsung.

The purpose of *A Voice from Inside* (particularly Chapters 5 and 6) is to contribute to the growing awareness of RTS by providing a discussion of the peculiarities of this condition among those who choose to stay. I hope to do this with the first-person account of my experience with RTS and subsequent recovery while maintaining active membership as a JW. I provide more information about the PIMO decision to stay in Chapter 6. To be clear, I neither recommend nor discouraged such a decision. But as I will show, it is a daily reality for many. And I wish to bring light to it.

The Author's Story

It is with regard to the principles of objectivity and transparency that I am compelled to reveal my hand in this discussion. It is natural for those who have been in abusive relationships to experience intense anger over the humiliation and betrayal that they experience. Expressing such anger constructively is a crucial step in their recovery from trauma. Along with anger can come an overwhelming desire to be vindicated for the moral appropriateness of one's actions in defense of self. However, with professional psychiatric and psychotherapeutic support, one can move past such bitterness to a transcendent equanimity void of any feelings of ill will toward one's fellow man, even a former oppressor.

This is the spiritual journey upon which I find myself.

All of this is to say: it is challenging for me to settle upon a tone for this volume. Loyalty to my spiritual community extends beyond my doctrinal disagreements and ethical conflict. Despite my disillusionment and subsequent trauma, I feel this loyalty still. And my current spiritual journey to equanimity serves to restrain me from lashing out vengefully against WTS, the Governing Body, or JWs in general. That being said, my experience with RTS was profound. The precariousness of my situation cannot be understated. Anyone who has experienced PTSD, with its accompanying panic attacks, intrusive thoughts, and uncontrollable suicidal ideation for months or years upon end, will understand that I am not exaggerating when I say that the situation is a matter of life and death.

I was raised "in the truth." This is an expression that insiders use to refer to someone whose parents raised them with JW beliefs and full involvement in congregation and evangelization activities. My comeuppance is similar to that of many of my JW peers: getting baptized in my early teens, forgoing post-secondary education, becoming a full-time proselytizer shortly after high school, and being appointed as a congregation elder in my late twenties. Beyond this, I was heavily involved in both attending and instructing specialized schools and training programs sponsored by WTS. I will remain vague about some of my higher-profile responsibilities to protect my anonymity. (More about the reasons for this precaution in the next section.)

Needless to say, a process of spiritual awakening brought the onset of RTS symptoms. The condition was unknown to me at the time. But as the symptoms of my trauma expanded over weeks and months, I began to recognize that what I was experiencing was meaningful; and meaningful not just for me. I started noticing similarities between my crisis and that of other members that I had heard about only from gossiping whispers in the backs of minivans while engaging in the door-to-door ministry. Memories of personal friends who had committed suicide and stories of others who had done the same came back to my mind with unexpected ferocity.

They were children, mothers, fathers.

After realizing the healing potential of my personal experience to others besides myself and noticing the general lack of awareness in the secular and academic community at the time, I started journaling. I have included some of my journal entries from the autumn of 2017 through the spring of 2019 to make the experience of RTS as a JW PIMO more relatable for my readers. Despite my best efforts, the intense grief I experienced over the loss of my God and my deeply held religious beliefs may make its way through to the tone of my writing. It is possible that residual bitterness and anger may raise their ugly heads in this volume.

But this book is not all about me. I am okay. Thanks for asking. I have an excellent team of mental health professionals who are patiently guiding me past my trauma and support me as I attempt to manifest self-actualization while navigating the complexities of living as a PIMO in an NRM.

The reality is that thousands besides me have experienced the life-altering symptoms of PTSD. And for those who cannot use the rejuvenating quality of spirituality as a tool for recovering from trauma (because it was at the very root of their trauma), I feel intense empathy. RTS can occur in any religious group that approaches the cultic pole on the spectrum of psychological and organizational captivity. Notorious examples of closed religious communities come to mind: The Church of Scientology, the Church of Jesus Christ of Latter-Day Saints, orthodox Judaism, radical Islamist groups, and hundreds of exploitative guru–devotee relationships in India and beyond. I want those suffering RTS while feeling trapped in their religious organizations to know that they are not alone. Further, for family members and friends who are concerned for the welfare of their loved ones who are associated with an ideologically totalist environment, I seek to deepen their insight into the challenges of the situation.

I also hope that readers will see the further application of these principles to other social, political and ideological movements. In the final chapters of this book, I will extend the principles of maintaining psychological independence inside an NRM to anyone who finds themselves captive in an ideologically totalist environment. Sometimes, we are all compelled to choose between the full expression of our individual and spiritual values and maintaining loving relationships with family and friends who subscribe to inflexible ideological stances.

Sometimes, we are all PIMOs.

Darkspilver and the Necessity of Anonymity

Readers might feel that the anonymity I employ is needlessly aggrandizing and symptomatic of a kind of paranoia that is all too common among individuals in authoritarian environments. But recent legal action from the Watchtower Bible & Tract Society's legal team, aimed at uncovering the identity of a PIMO dissenter on an online discussion forum of over 34,000 ex-JWs and PIMOs, shows that my caution is warranted. I am concerned that organizational leadership may proactively uncover and disfellowship me, a PIMO who choose to voice their criticisms of WTS. This brings me to the story of an anonymous JW Reddit user known only as Darkspilver.

Darkspilver was "raised in the truth" but began to question some of the teachings of his family religion. So, he shared some of his concerns on the ex/JW Reddit page. His grievances were connected with the organization's practices of eliciting funds from active members. JWs often praise their organization for how removed they are from exploitative financial practices common in mainstream Christianity, including passing the plate at church services and telemarketing campaigns. Darkspilver posted an image with the caption "What Gift Can We Give Jehovah?" (Watch Tower, 2018a) that appeared on the back of an issue of *Watchtower* magazine. He stated that he posted the image "to spark discussion about the organization's tone, message, and fundraising practices" and to demonstrate a "major change from the teaching and practices the Jehovah's Witnesses had espoused in the past" (Kim, 2019). Additionally, Darkspilver posted a chart that described the kind of personal information that WTS maintains about all their members, including advanced medical directives (what JWs call a "Blood Card") and judicial meeting reports (more about the congregation disciplinary procedures in Chapter 2).

The WTS legal team took Reddit, Inc. to court for breach of copyright laws. According to the presiding justice, Darkspilver's criticisms were protected under fair use copyright law. But during the proceedings, the WTS legal team subpoenaed Darkspilver's personal identity. Darkspilver felt that the effort by WTS to lift the mask of his anonymity was so that, regardless of the outcome of the court case, he could be held in violation of the organization's apostasy laws and brought before a judicial committee. The WTS legal team denied this, stating that they were not Darkspilver's local church and did not have the power to excommunicate him. The judge did not contest this statement.

Nevertheless, the court recognized that exposing the anonymous Reddit user's identity would severely limit his right to anonymous free speech. Highlighting the social repercussions that could result from his exposure, the court decided that "Darkspilver has demonstrated significant harms if his identity were revealed publicly or even if it were revealed to Jehovah's Witnesses in his congregation" (Kim, 2019). Darkspilver was certainly critical of his family religion online and probably no longer believed that WTS is the earthly representation of God's heavenly organization, but at the time he was not resolved to formally disassociate and giving up his family and friends forever.

Darkspilver appealed the subpoena for his identity. In the final outcome, the judge decided that the subpoenaed request for the personal identity of Darkspilver was necessary to the copyright law infringement suit leveled by WTS. However, conceding the reality of Darkspilver's concerns over the harm that could come to him from the powerful religious organization and the possibility that they could proactively disfellowship him, the judge stipulated: "only attorneys of record in this matter may obtain information about Darkspilver's identity. Watch Tower's attorneys of record shall not disclose Darkspilver's identity to anyone else without approval in a Court Order from this Court" (Kim, 2019)

With support from an understanding legal team at Reddit, Darkspilver's identity remains anonymous to this day.

The actions of the WTS legal team in Darkspilver's case shed light on my decision to withhold my identity. It is my opinion that WTS is not above using the full extent of the law to uncover dissenters, remove them from the religion, and coerce their family members into shunning them in perpetuity. For this reason, my name along with the names of all other characters in my memoir and journal entries have been changed to protect their identities.

But before I dive into my personal experience with RTS and my observations of the phenomenon from my perspective as a critical insider, it's important to understand a bit about the history and background of WTS and the pivotal moments in the organization's history that have led to the atmosphere that exists today.

2. Chronicling Captivity: The Path Toward High Control

Western religions are, at their foundation, systems of societal organization with mythological support for group norms of conduct. Religious doctrines of all kinds sanctify the biological predisposition of *Homo sapiens* toward in-group loyalty and out-group hostility. Given that JWs are also a community of *Homo sapiens* with mythologically based social norms, therefore, nothing is particularly outstanding about them. That WTS doctrine and policy create a legalistic community at odds with surrounding groups makes it, anthropologically speaking, unremarkable. The predicament of JWs is just an extreme version of the banal sociological tendencies of the human species. Many of the issues facing JW PIMOs today are present in religion on the whole, particularly the Abrahamic faiths. After discussing some of the psychological effects of these faiths in general, this section seeks to identify pivotal moments in WTS history that marked shifts toward the environment of captivity that exists in the organization today.

Psychological Captivity in Western Religion

The roots of modern Abrahamic religions hail from the agricultural revolution 10,000 years ago. The agricultural revolution marks a transition from the nomadic hunter-gatherer lifestyle of earlier generations to that of human domestication. For the first time in the evolution of man, humans were staying put. This called for more complex infrastructure. Societies organized the production of plant-based food into crops, storing grain as insurance for periods of drought or famine. They organized indigenous animal species into herds and flocks. And they organized themselves around collective mythology and ideology, developing religious systems that were much more elaborate than the animist beliefs of earlier epochs.

The religious mythology that evolved at this time was designed to support the domestication of humans within the boundaries of these early settlements. Religion morphed from a mystical quest for a deeper understanding of the spiritual curiosities of life, into the legalistic and moralistic codes of conduct associated with the Abrahamic religions today. Belief in an omniscient and omnipotent God was leveraged by lawmakers in these early civilizations to legitimize their policies for an orderly society. Among these early legalistic frameworks is the Mosaic law as recorded in the Bible books of Leviticus and Deuteronomy, upon which the moralistic religions are based—including Judaism, Christianity, and Islam. It is only since the scientific revolution and the Enlightenment of the sixteenth and eighteenth centuries that humankind has begun the process of deconstructing mythological morality in favor of more ubiquitous principles of humanism.

Some psychological challenges affect organized religion on the whole. The weaknesses of such religious philosophy have been adequately highlighted by the proponents of the New Atheism movement, including the likes of Richard Dawkins, Sam Harris, and Christopher Hitchens. Indeed, the failings of the Abrahamic religions extend far beyond members of fundamentalist groups like JWs. Given their multigenerational influence in the West, the psychological residue of the Abrahamic faiths remains in the deepest levels of the Western psyche and continues to impact social and political infrastructure.

Central to understanding the psychological captivity proliferated by the Abrahamic faiths is their legalistic nature. Christianity, Judaism, and Islam focus on morality, prescribing a standard of right and wrong and a list of dos and don'ts that inform the life choices of adherents. These religions base an entire system of ethics on supernatural myth. The result of this insistence upon accountability to a supernatural being limits the ever-evolving quest of the truly spiritual seeker.

The idea that actions can be wrong or right, good or bad, hated by God or acceptable to him restricts not only human behavior but also cognitive potential. In *The Evolving Self: A Psychology for the Third Millennium*, Mihaly Csikszentmihalyi discusses the psychological implications of nature's evolutionary tendency toward complexity (Csikszentmihalyi, 1993). Just as biological phonemes bifurcate toward the appearance of ever-diversifying species, so the meme-pool of the collective human consciousness bifurcates infinitely toward ever more nuanced and complex cognition. This evolution of human thought is at the heart of all scientific, technological, and sociopolitical progress. Any rigid system of belief or morality, such as religion, presents the potential to truncate this bifurcation with disallowable thought. When a thought is repressed based on the thinker's assumption that its presence in awareness is symptomatic of their inherent sinfulness or disapproval by God, entire architectures of thought remain unmanifested in consciousness. So do any subsequent architectures derived from them, ad infinitum. This presents an astounding opportunity cost when multiplied by the billions of human minds held captive by religious belief systems and restricted from reaching their creative potential.

The concept of belief in God as a delusion in the mind of the monotheist is outlined famously by Richard Dawkins in *The God Delusion* (Dawkins, 2006). While even Dawkins himself cannot admit to one hundred percent atheism (personally, I am closer to level five on his one-through-seven scale of agnosticism), surely living a life based on incessant servitude to a supernatural power in the pursuit of miraculous favor would indeed constitute a delusion of sorts. If not outright delusion, it certainly qualifies as fantastic thinking—the kind of thinking that Carl Jung (although a believer himself) identified as necessary to deconstruct as part of the self's progression from infantile fantasy to psychological maturity (Jung, 1966). While such a process inherently requires disappointment and disillusionment, as Jung brings out, it is a required step in the path toward greater psychic stability.

The Abrahamic faiths are more than spiritual pursuits. They confuse the conscientious pursuit of the mysteries of the universe (spirituality) with principles of human resource management. Mosaic Judaism and the religions that grew from it are systems of government, theocracies with a ruling priesthood made up of the types of men who are creative and courageous enough to claim inspiration from God and motivate societal change. While Jesus of Nazareth did much to reduce the oppression of this legalistic theocracy in his reform of Judaism, he failed to do so to the extent that his early followers did not repeat many of the mistakes of the previous generation of spiritual leaders.

Something similar can be said of the prophet Mohammed, who sought to create an idealized system of government based on the epitomic spiritual representations of his imagination. As seen in Islamic theocracies (and other utopian political ideologies such as communism) there is a disconnect between the imagination of devout men and the practical implementation of their ideologies. This is, of course, a challenge for visionaries and artists in general. The spiritual artist is by no means immune. An artist's skill resides largely in her ability to translate the idealized visions of her mind into a tangible or sensory work of art in the real world. Similarly, spiritual artists create visions of God and country and then attempt to implement them wholescale within their community. In this, they usually fail.

To the extent that Western religions are prescriptive and seek to teach a black-and-white version of right and wrong, they will be particularly damaging. In matters of sexuality for example (that are delineated clearly in The Holy Bible and The Holy Quran despite the best efforts of its more empathetic and progressive interpreters), Abrahamic religions allow only for heterosexual intercourse within the confines of a religio-social institution of marriage. These religions do not allow for the spectrum of gender and sexual expression that we see in modern culture. This is just one example of black-and-white thinking enshrined in Western religion.

This is not the case with the more transcendent philosophies of Eastern religions such as Buddhism, and Daoism. For example, at least one purpose of Daoist meditation is the de-categorization of the mind. Rather than restricting cognitive expansion (as in the case of black-and-white moral dogma), Daoist meditation promotes creativity and pairs nicely with Csikszentmihalyi's theory of the self that evolves toward greater complexity. Similarly, in the less dogmatic versions of Buddhism, despite the fantasticality of some of the associated religious mythology, the morality of adherents is not derived from religious doctrine. That is not to say that traditional cultural norms have not been intertwined with religious practice and become restrictions on human psychological potential. But while the moralistic nature of the Abrahamic faiths is fundamental to their systems, it is less so in Eastern religious philosophy.

Pivotal Moments in the Path to High Control

It has been said that all religions begin as cults. The *Oxford English Dictionary* defines a cult as "a system of religious veneration and devotion directed toward a particular figure or object" (Simpson & Weiner, 1989). Certain qualities predispose a man to such a cult-like following of disciples. Not the least of these is spirituality in its purest sense. Beyond this: confidence in the face of entropy, the ability to use eye contact, voice inflection, and body language to arouse motivating emotional responses in others, and sufficient imagination to construct a compelling ideology that fills gaps in the accepted mythology and addresses the most urgent biological and psychological deficiencies of the masses. Doubtless, among the ranks of historical characters who possessed these qualities were Abraham, Moses, Jesus of Nazareth, Mohammed, and Charles Taze Russell, the founder of Zion's Watch Tower Tract Society.

The question of whether a spiritual movement continues upon a path toward culthood or toward that of a more loosely organized religion lies in the ability of its leaders to integrate the community with society at large. How flexible and adaptable are the mythical stories? Can they absorb advancements in science and technology? Can they make room for conflicting cultures, belief systems, and political ideologies? To the extent that a religious leader gradually implements porosity upon the line of demarcation between the community of his followers and the larger society, a cult-like following evolves into a more liberal belief system that can coexist with surrounding institutions. To the extent that they do not, the group will be compelled to radicalize.

At pivotal moments in a spiritual movement's history, therefore, leaders will face a decision whether or not to reaffirm their beliefs and become rigid in their isolation and otherworldliness. Conversely, they have the rather uncomfortable option (but more sustainable in the long term) of revisiting their theology and fearlessly adapting to humanity's ever-increasing knowledge—be it knowledge of the physical laws of the universe from the domains of science or the hard-won historical lessons of human behavior.

These moments of decision are critical. Digging into existing doctrine and policy leads to ever-increasing separateness and radicalization. As evidenced throughout history, this presents grave consequences for humanity. Commendably, some progressive Judeo-Christian religions have twisted and contorted their doctrine to allow better integration with evolving human knowledge and experience. One thinks of the theological gymnastics that modern Protestant Christians perform to reconcile the acceptance of homosexuals into their ranks and even into the clergy. While homosexuality is overtly condemned in modern translations of both the Old and New Testaments, and no scriptural argument can be leveled upon an impartial reader that Jesus of Nazareth would have publicly supported homosexuals, Christian groups have undergone the difficult task of maintaining their faith while readjusting to trends in tolerance.

Such social progress in a religious community, in the face of condemnation by the devout, requires a fearless acceptance of responsibility on the part of religious leaders, and a courageous recognition of their role in shaping the long-term well-being of their followers. The difficult process of religious maturation also requires that leadership reckon with their own insecurities, fears, and biases that have for so long been protected under a veil of religious piety. This is no easy task. The outcome, however, can have far-reaching benefits. In time, as religious leaders perform the above soul-searching, progressive religion is rendered largely benign (outside of the aforementioned creative opportunity cost resulting from truncated creative cognition).

Historically, WTS has faced pivotal moments that would yield to humanitarian progress on the one hand or religious conservativism on the other. However, time and again, JW leadership took the path of reaffirming their religious rigidity and other worldliness rather than moderating themselves and integrating with society at large. This refusal to bend, attributed to a deep fear of compromising their loyalty to their god Jehovah, compelled them to dig in.

The result has been the ideologically totalist environment that JWs experience today and the accusations by many of culthood.

The following section attempts to identify these historically pivotal moments. This timeline is provided so that outsiders can understand the specific doctrinal and organizational moments that led a small spiritual movement of the late nineteenth century to become what they are today. For the insider, this section will read like historical revisionism. Although the following developments are specific to JWs and present a micro-focused version of their history as it relates to the journey toward their current organizational state, I hope that it will also serve as an object lesson for societal movements of all kinds—a sort of cautionary tale for those who find themselves in positions of leadership.

Charles Taze Russel & the Religious Post-Liberation Vacuum

Disillusionment with the religion of one's birth often leads to a post-religious-liberation spiritual vacuum wherein an individual challenges the only worldview they have ever known and gradually, often systematically, reconstructs a set of spiritual or religious values. I will further discuss how being unexpectedly thrust into this vacuum may cause the onset of RTS in Chapter 5—but it appears very likely that Charles Taze Russell also found himself in this spiritual vacuum. Whether his experience was accompanied by the symptoms of PTSD, I do not know – but the traditional insider narrative of Russell's disillusionment with religion could indeed be interpreted through the lens of religious trauma. Having suffered intense psychological suffering over the loss of his mother and siblings to early deaths, he began questioning what he saw as the tired platitudes of his religion and began his journey of faith deconstruction.

Russel took particular offense at the doctrine of eternal hellfire for the wicked and began the process of deconstructing his Presbyterian belief system. According to the WTS narrative, C.T. Russell dabbled in Eastern religion but found nothing to his liking. However, he failed to release his superstitious clutch on the Bible as the unaltered work of God. He viewed this book as the only reliable anchor to his faith. So then, Charles Taze Russell and a group of his trusted friends set about taking a fresh look at the scriptures. They would use only the Holy Bible for interpretation and would challenge all the existing beliefs of Christendom at the time. According to JWs, these events led to the reemergence of spiritual truth in the last days and sync perfectly with Bible prophecy and chronology.

However, secular history sheds some additional light and adds some perspective. Russell and his followers were part of a larger movement in nineteenth-century America called Adventism. (For an excellent discussion of the parallels between current JW doctrine and the Adventist movement, see Chryssides' *Jehovah's Witnesses: Continuity and Change*.)

It is far from uncommon for the spiritually disillusioned to make the mistake of repeating the leadership errors of their oppressors. For example, it was against exploitation and the misuse of power that the reformist Martin Luther composed and proliferated the Ninety-Five Theses. While movements like Luther's and Russell's appear at first to be incremental steps toward freedom from oppressive religion, far too often the search for spiritual freedom proceeds cyclically to new iterations of all too familiar circumstances.

In sum, freedom from spiritual oversight creates an ideological vacuum that ex-adherents, in their worldly immaturity, crave to have filled. It requires a certain ease with mystery and chaos on the part of a spiritual guide to resist the urge to reintroduce organization and structure into the spiritual quest. Russel did not resist that urge. In 1879, he published the first copy of *Zion's WatchTower & Herald of Christ's Presence*. Later, he formed Zion's Watch Tower Tract Society.

In a sociological study of Jehovah's Witnesses titled *The*

Trumpet of Prophecy, James A. Beckford provides insight into the next step toward High Control. He highlights a shift in Russell's thinking in 1881 when his earliest prediction of the heavenly rapture of God's loyal servants failed to materialize (or should I say, dematerialize). From 1881 onwards, faced with responsibility for the disciples he had gathered to himself, Russel turned his attention toward organizing the Russellites, as early followers of Russell were pejoratively called. In addition to adding structure to the community in the United States, he also increased his focus on the expansion of his version of Adventist doctrine abroad. Met with the realities of his continued presence on the material earth, Pastor Russell was forced to face his leadership obligations to the movement that he had created. According to Beckford, in the ensuing years Russell "sanctioned the formation of local 'ecclesias' for his followers" and "began to exercise increasingly effective control over their structure and functions" (Beckford, 1975, p.8). As Beckford puts it, the doctrinal and organizational developments in the last two decades of the 1800s "precipitated a feeling of collective identity among Russellites which, in turn, was a measure of increasing responsibility for them that Zion's Watch Tower Tract Society was assuming: it had ceased to function merely as a publishing enterprise" (Beckford, 1975, p. 9).

So while Russell, reacting to what he saw as a distancing from spiritual truth by mainstream religion, claimed initially to be disinterested in formalizing a religious institution, he ended up collecting followers to himself and began a movement that would later become Jehovah's Witnesses. As is so often the case with immature leadership, Russell set in motion elements of order and control that would lead to even greater captivity for future generations. I am reminded of twentieth-century British philosopher Bertrand Russell's comments about French syndicalists, who revolting under the banner of anarchism, but soon found themselves without adequate leadership for a government and "without the required training because of their previous abstention from politics," (Russell, 1917). Because of this inexperience, they were compelled to form an administration that violated the very values of the movement. Similarly, Charles Taze Russell, seeking to remove the yoke of oppressive religion with its dominating clergy, found himself in the post-liberation spiritual vacuum and subsequently caused a chain of events that led to the creation of what would later be referred to as a captive organization.

Theocratization and Theocratic Warfare

Following the death of Charles Taze Russell in 1916, the second president of WTS, Joseph F. Rutherford, instituted several crucial changes to the doctrine and policy of the Bible Students (as Russellites later became known) that had grave implications for the future of the movement. The impact that Rutherford's brazen seizure of power and control had upon the group's future as an HDRG cannot be understated.

In his insider history *Faith on the March* published in 1957, early Bible Student and personal secretary to Charles Russell, A.H. Macmillan, interprets the dramatic changes brought by the Rutherford administration in a manner that is repeated by devout JWs to this day. In

Macmillan's account of the announcement of Rutherford's death in 1942 at a congregation in Virginia, USA, he says the following:

> J.F. Rutherford had been loved and was missed. But he had, himself, worked diligently to tear out the very roots of creature worship or dependency of the organization on individuals (…) None said, "What are we going to do now?" or "How will things go?" (…) none expressed doubts or fears as to what his passing might mean to the organization.
>
> That was typical of the reaction of all of Jehovah's Witnesses. As members of a theocratic organization, we now realized the work would continue as the Lord directed, regardless of whoever might be taking the lead on earth. Rutherford had continually expressed that thought in The Watchtower; and by the time he died all associated in the work, including those of the headquarters staff had become more stabilized and mature in their thinking. Although Rutherford was a vigorous and prominent figure in the organization, yet his somewhat sudden death caused no great upheaval in the work, as it would have if we had been following a man (Macmillan, 1957, p.196).

In the above quote, Macmillan addresses the evolution of the Bible Students' theology from discipleship of Charles Taze Russell ("creature worship") to citizenship of a theocracy that would "continue as the Lord directed, regardless of whoever might be taking the lead on earth." This shift was seen as a positive change that would ensure that the movement would develop according to the supernatural direction of the divine source, and not according to the corruptible decisions of man. The result, however, was the reintroduction introduction of mystical manipulation by a WTS leadership (one of Lifton's 8 elements of ideologically totalist communities that I will discuss further in Chapter 3) but in a different form: "The Society". In the minds of the Bible Students, "The Society" became the instrument of God's communication with humankind in modern times.

This is an excellent example of a psychological tendency of *Homo sapiens* that Yuval Noah Harari discusses in his book *Sapiens*: the capacity of imbuing legal corporations with powers and characteristics based solely on collective imagination. Anthropomorphism of corporations results from "telling stories, and convincing people to believe them" (Harari, 2016). Humans do this so well, says Harari, that "we forget they exist only in our imagination."

> Ever since the cognitive revolution, Sapiens have thus been living in a dual reality. On the one hand, the objective reality of rivers, trees and lions; and on the other hand, the imagined reality of gods, nations and corporations. As time went by, the imagined reality became ever more powerful, so that today the very survival of rivers, trees and lions depends on the grace of imagined entities such as the United States and Google (Harari, 2016)

Devout JWs live in such a dual reality—the imagined, albeit very convincing, reality wherein their salvation rests upon obedience to instructions published by the Watch

Tower Bible & Tract Society of Pennsylvania Incorporated and the Governing Body of Jehovah's Witnesses.

Rutherford began a process of "theocratising" (Chryssides, 2016, p.130) the organization to centralize control of all congregations under the authority of WTS. By means of changes to rhetorical tone, doctrine and policy, Rutherford "succeeded in creating a high level of doctrinal orthodoxy among his followers" and "persuaded most of them of the need to be unselfishly energetic in centrally organized 'service work'" (Beckford, 1975, p. 33) in support of the movement. The effect of these forces upon the psychology of the modern JW is palpable.

Although, as Macmillan says, Rutherford's theocratization meant that no single man could be fingered as the leader of a cult of Bible students, Rutherford's writings and leadership marked a change in the tone of WTS rhetoric that reinforced the group's segregation from society at large. Rutherford's work can rightly be called propaganda, "the use of biased or misleading information to manipulate the way people think and act" (Watch Tower, 2017a, p.27). Rutherford created "a grand theory of Satan's conspiracy against the attempts of Bible Students" (Beckford, 1975, p.28) to save people of the world from impending doom at Armageddon. Rutherford's "acerbic tone" drove a wedge between the Bible Students and outsiders, creating "a sense of belonging to a distinctive body which was in important respects at odds with its environing society" (Beckford, 1975, p.29).

Rutherford set about differentiating the organization. The name Bible Students was not a strong enough identifier for the movement. In 1931, Rutherford changed their name to Jehovah's Witnesses, providing adherents with the strong sense of spiritual elitism that many have noted during their doorstep visits to this day. Many JWs are of the belief that Isaiah 43:10 refers to their very organization by name when it says,

> You are my witnesses, declares Jehovah,
>
> Yes, my servant whom I have chosen.
>
> (Watch Tower, 2013a)

Rutherford also chose the name Kingdom Hall to refer to the buildings where Jehovah's Witnesses meet. This furthered feelings of separateness from mainstream Christianity. Even now, it is not uncommon to be corrected by a JW coworker when referring to their Sunday morning scheduling restriction as "church".

"Oh, sorry," you check your political correctness, "I meant *Kingdom Hall.*"

But it was a two-part series of articles in the *Watchtower*, appearing in 1938, that shifted the culture of Jehovah's Witnesses permanently. The series was titled "Organization". It was pivotal in changing the structure of Jehovah's Witnesses from a loose network of congregations around the world to a formally organized religion with centralized authority at headquarters in New York City. The series "Organization" included a draft declaration of commitment that every congregation was given the opportunity to sign and return to WTS headquarters. It read as follows:

> We, the company of God's people taken out for his name, and now at -------- recognize that God's government is a pure theocracy and that Christ Jesus is at the temple and in full charge and control of the visible organization of Jehovah, as well as the invisible, and that "THE SOCIETY" is the visible representative of the Lord on earth, and we therefore request "The Society" to organize this company for service and to appoint the various servants thereof, so that all of us may work together in peace, righteousness, harmony and complete unity. We attach hereto a list of names of persons in this company that to us appear more fully mature and who therefore appear to be best suited to fill the respective positions designated for service. (Watch Tower, 1938, p. 182)

This centralization of the organization has only strengthened with the passing of decades. The Governing Body of Jehovah's Witnesses, with offices in Warwick, New York, USA, oversees over 100,000 congregations all over the world. Today records of each JW are kept under record at headquarters in New York, much like employees of a company. The organization maintains copious personal records of even rank-and-file members, including names, dates of birth, baptism dates, congregations attended, and records of disciplinary action taken for behavioral violations. Darkspilver alluded to such records in his post on Reddit. This same organizational record-keeping has led to the accusation in 2019 in *The Atlantic* magazine of a "secret database of child abuse" held by WTS. Legal representatives of ex-JWs alleging sexual abuse during their time with WTS are struggling to access disciplinary records of child sexual abusers maintained by the organization that have not been shared with law enforcement agencies for the protection of the greater community (Quenqua, 2019). When I was in the initial stages of RTS, the authority of the organization over my personal life and their records of my private information contributed to a state of deep fear that was not unlike paranoia. This may also be the case for many other disillusioned JWs with RTS

Rutherford's vitriolic tone ended with his death and the inauguration of WTS's third president, Nathan H. Knorr. However, the religious doctrines underpinning out-group hostility remain unaltered among many JWs to this day. The theology of fear and disgust for outside religion, fomented by Rutherford's propaganda, remains. Rutherford called all religion a "snare and a racket" and "unchristian". Eventually, WTS conceded that they too fit the definition of the term religion. So, from 1951 onward, "the expressions 'true religion' and 'false religion' became common among Jehovah's Witnesses" (Watch Tower, 1976, p. 225). This unperforated line of demarcation in the minds of JWs between true and false religion still exists today.

Devout JWs believe that they are engaged in theocratic warfare "against wicked spirit forces in the heavenly places" (Ephesians 6:12; Watch Tower, 2013a). They believe that they are soldiers in a spiritual battle against the religious, political, and social elements of a world under demonic control. WTS teaches that God has charged JWs with a ministry that "enlightens the people against the forces of darkness, which represent wickedness" and that an individual "agrees to engage in this spiritual battling when he dedicates his life to God"(Watch Tower, 1976, p. 225). Therefore, any argument from outsiders based on religious or secular ideology is interpreted may well be interpreted as an attack from Satan. In the minds of loyal JWs, even non-believing family members can unwittingly be used by the Wicked One to distract them from their service to God.

Current State: Doctrine and Policy that Contributes to Captivity

The above developments show how the wanderings of a newly liberated spiritual seeker like Charles Taze Russel can evolve into religious authoritarianism. Over the decades, WTS leaders chose to reaffirm their organization's religious rigidity rather than moderate their doctrine and integrate with the global community's progress toward the protection of fundamental human rights of citizens. In the face of the progressive societal changes of modernity, WTS has responded by doubling down on problematic doctrine and policy.

In *The Trumpet of Prophecy*, Beckford mentions a relaxation of the organization's "extreme hostility towards all non-Watch Tower aspects of life" with Nathan H. Knorr's administration in the 1940s. Knorr's leadership was a "new-found orientation towards internationalism" evidenced by large international conventions and an acceleration of the evangelical work worldwide. Jehovah's Witnesses came to "think of themselves collectively as an international movement" (Beckford, 1975, p. 51). This concept of loyalty to a united worldwide brotherhood is strong among JWs today. The collective consciousness of this international family is seen in WTS's impressive translation efforts, the brightly colored and multicultural videos presented at meetings and assemblies, and the international wanderings of many JW twenty-somethings in the west to less developed countries with a desire for the exciting missionary life.

Nevertheless, despite the gradual softening of rhetoric, the worldwide education efforts during the Knorr administration proliferated many of the doctrines that led to the hostile separateness of the early Bible Students in the United States. And because modern JWs can still find a scriptural basis for their traditional beliefs, there has been very little moderating of the theology at the root of allegations of organizational captivity today. The following section will outline some of the most impactful doctrinal contributors to the current psychosocial state of WTS.

You Are No Part of the World (John 15:19)

Central to all discrimination and prejudice is polarized in-group/out-group thinking. To the extent that this is a biological inclination of the human species, it may be unavoidable. However, it is one thing to reckon with our implicit biases and endeavor to base our actions on equanimity to the best of our ability. It is quite another to deliberately proliferate divisive ideology.

The teaching that JWs must be "no part of the world" falls into the latter category. JWs are quick to highlight that their unified international brotherhood suffers neither from racial nor economic classism. But religious intolerance is an explicit part of the organization's theology. The fact that this teaching originates with Jesus of Nazareth does not excuse it. JWs consider themselves first and foremost to be citizens of God's Kingdom, a heavenly government operating beyond the realm of existing political regimes. Loyalty to this kingdom is paramount.

In the second of two textbooks required for completion before baptism called *Keep Yourself In God's Love*, a chapter called "How to Keep Separate From the World," provides scriptural principles to help new converts maintain their loyalty. Among the ways to remain separate from the world discussed in this chapter are neutrality in politics, rejecting an independent spirit, living a simple life, and suggestions on how to "subordinate our presumed rights to the consciences of others" in one's choice of clothing and hairstyles. Citing the Bible book of Ephesians, Satan is called "the ruler of the authority of the air" (Ephesians 6:12; Watch Tower, 2013a).

> The world's "air", or spirit, is an invisible, impelling force that incites disobedience to God (…) Simply put, the spirit of the world progressively causes the traits of the Devil to grow in the hearts of humans (Watch Tower, 2014a, p.54)

There is no gray area here. You are either one of Jehovah's

Witnesses, or you are part of a world under the influence of the Devil. This teaching inculcates in members an extreme distrust of all outside voices and nurtures a deep fear of the world outside the confines of the organization.

Interestingly, this is often the first doctrine deconstructed by awakening JWs. As with all prejudice, emotional empathy for members of the out-group can bring down the walls of bias. Sometimes while at school or work, a JW is subject to a level of emotional connectedness that they cannot ignore. Greater human laws of empathy and understanding pierce through years of indoctrination. In time, the outsider begins to look more like themselves than they expected. In other cases, a bad experience within the brotherhood can cause a JW to question the moral and spiritual superiority of JWs as the chosen people of God.

JWs describe themselves as beneficial contributors to the community. They claim that teaching people about the Bible's standards on sexuality, drunkenness and drug abuse creates better members of the community and stronger families. (I will restrain myself from any utilitarian philosophical debate as to whether the advantages of forced compliance to a moral code exceed the psychological damage brought by disfellowshipping, enforced shunning, and the proliferation of bias). But it is my opinion as an insider that for many devout JWs, a deep-seated prejudice against disinterested non-members remains hidden from conscious awareness. If outsiders refuse the opportunity to accept their message, this hostility may raise its ugly head. From personal experience, I can attest that it was not uncommon during the 1990s and early 2000s to hear JWs refer to disinterested neighbors as "goats" fit for destruction (based on Jesus' parable of separating the sheep from the goats in Matthew chapter 25). In those days, when JWs were ridiculed during their door-to-door ministry, bitter comments about the fate of the disinterested individual at Armageddon would be recited in car groups by JW preachers. Although this practice seems to have moderated in recent years, the doctrines underpinning the hostility remain unchanged.

Dedication & Baptism

In the midst of my trauma, I remember thinking about how WTS leadership might go about creating a solution to the allegations of psychological and organizational captivity. I thought: what is the opposite of disfellowshipping? If disfellowshipping is the forced removal of a member for non-compliance and subsequent alienation from all social support including blood relatives, then the opposite must be any organizational mechanism that commits someone to this policy. That organizational mechanism is baptism. Without baptism, there would be no need for disfellowshipping.

Baptism of course is not unique to Jehovah's Witnesses; it is a common sacrament of many Christian faiths. But baptism for a JW represents a formalized entrance into the organization. The theology of baptism among JWs produces a psychological state of subordination to the organization and a contractual relationship, including articulated repercussions for breach.

It is important to mention that undue social influence does not begin at baptism. Even unbaptized publishers (members who attend congregation meetings and join in evangelization efforts but who are not yet baptized) are subject to the code of conduct and disciplinary procedures of the organization. Details on how to handle reports of unacceptable conduct appear in the handbook for congregation elders called *Shepherd the Flock of God*. Although a formal "judicial committee" of three congregation elders is not formed in cases of misconduct by unbaptized publishers, policy requires that "the body of elders should select two elders to meet with him." If the unbaptized publisher's "wrongdoing" is deemed egregious enough, an announcement is made to congregations that "a matter involving [name of person] has been handled, and he [she] continues to serve as an unbaptized publisher." Or, if the individual doesn't show enough remorse to convince the elders that they have a contrite spirit, "[Name of person] is no longer recognized as an unbaptized publisher." This public shaming may also include "a scriptural talk about the sort of wrongdoing involved" that may be presented to the congregation "a few weeks after the announcement". The elders may also choose to make a private visit to JWs who are particularly close to the unbaptized publisher communicating with them the dangers of socializing with the offender (Watch Tower, 2019a).

This procedure seems particularly unfair for newly interested adults who have been brought into the Kingdom Hall through the evangelizing work. These individuals do not receive a copy of the code of conduct to which they will be held accountable until *after* the elders determine that they can qualify as unbaptized publishers. It is only *after* they have undergone the formal process of becoming an unbaptized publisher that the individual is "eligible to receive his own copy of *Organized to Do Jehovah's Will*" (Watch Tower, 2019a)— the very publication that articulates the code of conduct and disciplinary policy to which they will subsequently be held.

However, many unbaptized publishers are teen and preteen children of JW parents. At baptism, they enter into a contractual agreement with WTS to abide by a set of moral laws under the penalty of disfellowshipping and shunning. These minors hardly possess the psychological maturity to make decisions with such lifelong implications. Most local governments protect minors from entering long-term commitments for which they are unprepared. For example, legal commitment to marriage or financial obligations (like loans) often require an adult cosignatory if the applicant is under eighteen. No such requirement is made at baptism for formally ceding lifelong religious liberty to WTS. Furthermore, the behavioral requirements of the baptism contract are subject to unilateral amendment by WTS without opportunity for renegotiation on the part of individuals subject to the contract.

Organized to Do Jehovah's Will (Watch Tower, 2019b) states that baptism consists of two elements. One is the personal dedication to Jehovah that happens in private prayer, and the second is symbolizing this dedication by water baptism (p. 78). After performing a series of three interviews with congregation elders, the candidate is asked the following questions, initially before two congregation elders, and finally while standing before a crowd at a larger assembly of JWs.

> 1.　　　Have you repented of your sins, dedicated yourself to Jehovah, and accepted his way of salvation through Jesus Christ?

> 2.　　　Do you understand that your baptism identifies you as one of Jehovah's Witnesses in association with Jehovah's organization?

Baptism is of deep significance for JWs. Psychologically, it represents the death of the self and rebirth to a life of committed service to Jehovah God. This death of self at baptism contributes to what Beckford refers to as a "lack of focus on individual liberties" (Beckford, 1975) and the rendering of all personal goals, aspirations, and desires subordinate to the will of God as outlined by WTS leadership. A JW may well consider the date of their baptism as the most important day of their life, held in reverence above their date of birth, date of marriage, or the birth of a child. Date of baptism is often embossed in gold typeface on leather-bound Bibles and hymnbooks. And WTS headquarters confirms the identity of JW callers via baptism date (similar to how one might use their date of birth to confirm their identity at a financial institution).

WTS writers leverage an individual JW's desire to live up to their dedication as a way of discouraging dissent. An example of this comes from an article from the *Watchtower*, studied worldwide at a recent congregation meeting: "Recall that dedication is a vow and that Jehovah expects you to keep it. So after your baptism, you have to live up to your dedication." Another comes from the daily Bible text considered at the breakfast tables of JWs around the world on September 29th, 2020, reminding them that they "live a life of dedication 'as slaves of God'" (Watch Tower, 2020a).

"Not Even Eating with Such a Man" (1 Corinthians 5:11–13)

This brings us to disfellowshipping and enforced shunning. Disfellowshipping is by far the largest single contributor to allegations of captivity among JWs. To begin, an important distinction must be made between disfellowshipping and the practice of ex-communication in other Christian denominations. Excommunication is defined as "the action of officially excluding someone from participation in the sacraments and services of the Christian Church" (Simpson & Weiner, 1989). If an active member violates a fundamental tenet of the faith, official removal from the Church ensues. While the practice of ex-communication demonstrates the divisive potential of Christianity in general, disfellowshipping goes a step further.

The disfellowshipping policy is based on a scriptural passage found in the Bible at 1 Corinthians 5:11–13, written by Paul the Apostle:

> Stop keeping company with anyone called a brother who is sexually immoral or a greedy person or an idolater or a reviler or a drunkard or an extortioner, not even eating with such a man (…) Remove the wicked person from among

yourselves. (Watch Tower, 2013a)

The expanded edition of the *New World Translation of the Holy Scriptures: Study Edition* includes a non-canonical footnote to this verse stating that "'keeping company' with others would imply having close fellowship or companionship with them and sharing their views and sentiments." It explains that to "stop keeping company with" means that a Christian would "refuse to mingle" with an unrepentant sinner (Watch Tower, 2013a).

The practice of cutting off all communication with disfellowshipped ex-members can rightly be called shunning, however adamantly JWs disavow the application of the term to themselves. Although other Christian institutions find shunning needlessly cruel, there is enough verbiage in the New Testament to form a compelling argument for the practice. It was Jesus of Nazareth himself who said, "I came not to bring peace, but a sword" (Matthew 10:34; Watch Tower, 2013a) and foretold that his disciples would leave "house or brothers or sisters or mother or father or children" (Mark 10:29; Watch Tower, 2013a). for his sake. As damaging as these policies are, disfellowshipping and shunning are not categorically unchristian.

According to WTS policy, immediate family members who share a home together may continue to have everyday interaction as long as this does not involve spiritual conversation. But for family who do not share the same physical dwelling, "the situation is different." "It may be possible to have almost no contact at all with the relative" (Watch Tower, 2019b). The same policies apply for disassociation as outlined in the conversation between Angus Stewart and Geoffrey Jackson in the introduction to this book.

Further, shunning is enforced under the threat of disfellowshipping. The rank-and-file understand that if they are caught associating with an ex-member, they are likely to receive a visit from the congregation elders and could be disfellowshipped themselves.

"No Contact At All"

The authority bestowed upon congregation elders by the WTS to judge individual members as no longer worthy of association with their own blood relatives, and the power vested in them to enforce this policy by further disfellowshipping those who violate shunning rules, has considerable coercive force. If a baptized witness even considers behaving in a way that could get them disfellowshipped, they are encouraged to ask themselves, "What effect would the wrong action have on my family?" (Watch Tower, 2013b, p. 29). The immediate emotional response to this question is fear. In the mind of a devout JW, the answer to the above question is that they will be disfellowshipped and will break the hearts of everyone they love when they are expelled for their "wrong action". This encouragement to fearful self-examination and the resulting determination of devout JWs to avoid causing their loved ones pain creates a cognitive loop. 1) An errant desire or dissenting attitude enters consciousness, 2) a fear response is triggered at the thought of complete rejection by all social supports, and 3) the JW reaffirms their determination to uphold the moral standards of the organization. This cognitive pattern is at the heart of what psychologists call coercive persuasion.

As I discuss further in Chapter 6, outsiders often overlook the unspoken pain of remaining JWs after a family member is disfellowshipped or disassociates. Many times as a congregation elder, I comforted grieving mothers who had lost a child to disfellowshipping. Of course, their children were alive and well and longing to reconnect with their mother. In my ignorance, I contributed to this pain and coercion, putting my arm around the sobbing mother to assure her that her loyalty "makes Jehovah's heart glad" (Watch Tower, 2011a, p. 32).

It's heartbreaking.

Interestingly, an update was made to the most recent edition of the elder's manual, *Shepherd the Flock of God*, which offers hope for the moderation of this policy.

> If a publisher in the congregation is known to have unnecessary association with disfellowshipped or disassociated *relatives* who are not in the household, elders should use the Scriptures to counsel and reason with him (…) If it is clear that a Christian is violating the spirit of the disfellowshipping decree in this regard and does not respond to counsel, he would not qualify for congregation privileges, which require one to be exemplary (Watch Tower, 2019a)

It would seem from the above that the mother in my

previous example now has the option of forfeiting special privileges in the congregation (such as full-time evangelization work or volunteering for organizationally sponsored construction projects) in exchange for the opportunity to embrace her daughter again. However, this policy change was made the privy of elders only. Rank-and-file JWs are unaware of this loophole. It is published nowhere outside of the elder's manual. Additionally, elders, arguably the most obedient JWs, have no organizationally sanctioned means of communicating this change to the lay-witnesses whose families have been torn apart by the disfellowshipping policy.

Call the Older Men (James 5:14,15)

The scriptural basis for the disciplinary authority of congregation elders over rank-and-file JWs is weak indeed. While the organization claims to base this arrangement on the first-century Christian Church, very little scriptural evidence exists to support the legalistic disciplinary proceedings of Jehovah's Witnesses. The scriptural verse at James 5:14 appears often in WTS literature as the theological basis for compulsory confession to elders: "Is there anyone sick among you? Let him call the elders of the congregation to him, and let them pray over him (...) Also, if he has committed sins, he will be forgiven" (Watch Tower, 2013a).

From these sentiments comes the familiar concept of the confessional in mainstream Christianity. Surely, divulging one's deepest darkest secrets in the safety of a confessional booth or, for the secular among us, a psychotherapist's office, can be of tremendous cathartic value. Indeed, the *Watchtower* recommends the following action if one is plagued with guilt:

> A Christian guilty of serious sin needs to seek the help of congregation elders to recover (…) Elders are commissioned and trained to reassure repentant sinners, helping to ease their pain and guilt (…) Would you not agree that this arrangement is an expression of God's mercy? (Watch Tower, 2017b)

While private confession of personal transgressions to two elders can offer the aforementioned psychological release, the situation quickly turns on its head. Following the placating of troubled consciences, the elders must adjudicate the sin to determine the necessary disciplinary response. Elders are, indeed, "commissioned and trained" for this very purpose, and a large bulk of their specialized seminars center on the interpretation of what offenses meet the organization's threshold for the formation of a judicial committee.

Nobody is more aware of WTS jurisprudence than the congregation elder. It is not uncommon for lay-witnesses who are less aware of the gravity assigned to their behavioral infractions to humbly approach the elders to be forgiven and draw closer to God, only to end up with an unexpected judicial proceeding. So that they can ensure that their decisions are in harmony with Jehovah's direction, the elders tell the guilt-filled penitent, they will require more information about the sin. The next step is an interrogation of the guilty party about the details of the offense. The information elicited by the two investigating elders is then brought back to the entire body, who determine whether a judicial committee needs to be formed. This humiliating interchange occurs before the judicial proceedings even begin.

The judicial procedure consists of a three-elder body, called a judicial committee, who are charged with determining the level of repentance displayed by the offender. Before inviting the offender into the room, the judicial committee will convene to prepare themselves for the case, reviewing pertinent information from the elder's manual. They remind themselves of the Bible verse that gives them their judicial authority: "Pay attention to what you are doing, for you do not judge for man but for Jehovah, and he is with you when you pass judgment" (2 Chronicles 19:6,7; Watch Tower, 2013a).

There is invariably at least one elder on the committee who was not part of the initial investigation and has not yet heard the details of the event firsthand. Therefore, a repetition of the confession may be requested of the accused, and the judicial committee will probe further to glean any details not divulged in the initial confession and investigation. According to the elder's manual, the purpose of the judicial hearing is to determine "genuine repentance": "Repentance involves a deep regret over a damaged relationship with Jehovah, remorse over the reproach brought upon God's name and people, and a sincere longing to come back into Jehovah's favor" (Watch Tower, 2019a).

The elders then determine whether the repentance is "commensurate" with the gravity of the sin. This involves a balanced assessment of the guilty party's outward displays of remorse (tears, shame, apologies, etc.) and of any actions that demonstrate that they have ceased the unsanctioned behavior. WTS places emphasis on "sadness in a Godly way" (2 Corinthians 7:9; Watch Tower, 2013a) This means that the individual must display remorse for offending *Jehovah*, not remorse over potential punishment. Psychological enslavement to Jehovah is reinforced through shame and by the individual's recommitment to purity following the discipline received.

Finally, the elders excuse the offender from the room and deliberate amongst themselves while the powerless lay-witness, trembling, awaits their fate. If the elders determine that repentance is genuine and commensurate to the gravity of the transgression, they will formally discipline the individual. This discipline, called reproof, may be accompanied by restrictions on "privileges of service" like audience participation at meetings. If others inside or outside the congregation know about the transgression, reproof will be announced at the next mid-week meeting; "[name of member] has been reproved". However, even if reproof goes unannounced, the congregation is undoubtedly aware of the discipline as evidenced by the out-of-character silence of the guilty party at congregation meetings. Rumors and gossip proliferate.

However, if the individual is deemed unrepentant, they are disfellowshipped. Even if the accused feels remorseful, they may not be able to provide sufficient evidence of "genuine repentance" to convince the elders to allow them to remain a member of the congregation. Again, rank-and-file JWs do not have a clear understanding of the intricacies of what is required to prove their repentance, as do elders. The elder's manual puts it this way:

> keep in mind that if the wrongdoer has demonstrated few or no works of repentance before the judicial hearing is held, it may not be possible during the hearing to move him to demonstrate sufficient repentance to justify extending mercy. (Watch Tower, 2019a)

It is not enough just to show remorse. For example, imagine a twenty-year-old JW sobbing her eyes out in front of the elders because she had an exclusive sexual relationship with her boyfriend over the past six months. "But how many times did they do it?" the elders ask themselves. "Once a week? Once every two weeks? That's at least twelve violations?!" If the elders feel that the sin is too grave and too entrenched, no amount of crying or promising to improve will suffice. She will be disfellowshipped.

So it is that some individuals who approach the elders to ease their conscience before god and get a clean slate, unexpectedly find themselves disfellowshipped and shunned by their family and friends. In my experience, elders forget how little the rank and file know about the disciplinary proceedings. They are shocked that the offender is shocked that they have been disfellowshipped.

The whole process can be traumatic. Elders conduct themselves with the utmost seriousness and formality, morphing from your friendly fun-loving Saturday morning door-to-door ministry partner into the harbingers of your spiritual fate. The process can drag on for weeks. If printed direction from WTS does not directly address a nuance of the circumstance at hand, judicial committee elders, fearful of acting presumptuously and independently in what they consider to be God's work, may defer to the headquarters to weigh in on the judicial decision. This means that the committee must hold the matter in abeyance until the judicial committee elders can call WTS headquarters in New York during business hours, and subsequently convene the meeting to make a final decision.

The detrimental effect of this process on the psychological well-being of congregation members is highlighted by a section in the elder's handbook providing instructions under the heading "If the Accused Threatens Suicide." Even WTS recognizes that putting members through the judicial process can cause suicidal ideation. In cases where a guilty JW mentions suicide, the instructions allow for elders to postpone judicial proceedings to help the accused "regain his balance". The elder's manual instructs judicial committee members to "broach the subject of depression and suicide, using the Scriptures and Bible-based publications" at a later time (Watch Tower, 2019a). Although the restriction upon elders from recommending specific mental health resources is no longer mentioned in the latest version of the elder's manual (Watch Tower, 2012a, p.55), no direction from WTS requires elders to take responsibility for ensuring that a member of the flock gets professional immediate medical care for this life-threatening condition.

This chapter has focused on the history, theology, and policy of Jehovah's Witnesses that lead to allegations that it is a captive organization. But there is more to the story. As many social psychologists and ex-members alike have noticed, closed religious communities often have distinct psychosocial peculiarities. While often appearing mysterious and unfathomable to outsiders who have never experienced it, the mechanics of psychological captivity are predictable and repeatable. The following chapter will discuss this topic further in the context of Jehovah's Witnesses.

3. The Mechanics of Psychological Captivity

While potentially dangerous in extreme cases, social conformity is not unnatural; no matter how much our Western individualist minds make us cringe at the thought. At some level, social conformity affects us all. And that's okay. We all need a tribe to survive. Social connection is healthy for *Homo sapiens* and to be accepted by any social group we must, to a certain extent, conform to their prescribed behavioral norms. Given the ubiquity of these human psychosocial tendencies, nothing is particularly shocking or confusing about the social environment of JWs.

However, left unchecked by independent thought and criticism, conformity and obedience can lead to some fairly predictable challenges in closed communities. Groups members may begin to lose hold of their grasp on objective reality in favor of a collective consciousness reinforced by influential and authoritative leadership.

Whether or not a leader is maniacally and deliberately manipulating the psychological vulnerabilities of his or her followers is open to debate on a cult-by-cult basis. The frank truth is that even the most benign of human relationships contain subtle power dynamics and manipulation. If someone in a leadership position has mastered these psychological dark arts, they must set boundaries for their ethical usage or else be checked by a higher authority. On the other hand, an unaware manipulator can cause significant psychological damage to others. I believe that many manipulators exploit people unwittingly, succumbing to common egoistic traps that have befallen thousands of visionary and charismatic personality types throughout history.

Therefore, I do not sit in judgment of the motives of WTS leadership, including the Governing Body. I do not believe that they are performing deliberate sorcery over the minds of their subjects. One could hypothesize that they too, having a rich cultural history with the organization and deep faith in its tenets, are subject to the collective consciousness of their community and at the mercy of their own psychological blind spots.

As I mentioned in the introduction, I feel that the term "brainwashing" is overly simplistic and pejorative. That being said, accusations of brainwashing by outsiders are not without foundation. NRMs and HDRGs often have a distinct sociopsychological state that outsiders notice immediately. Many comment that insiders appear to have lost both their individuality and their ability to think critically about the movement to which they belong. In this chapter, I will attempt to explain this phenomenon as it appears in Jehovah's Witnesses by applying Robert Jay Lifton's eight criteria of ideological totalism (as outlined in *Losing Reality: On Cults, Cultism, and the Mindset of Political and Religious Zealotry*) to WTS. Further, I will argue that the ideological totalitarianism of WTS may increase the potential for a precipitous fall from the heights of dogmatic faith to the perilous lows of PTSD and RTS.

First, however, it is important to understand the identity of a group that plays a particularly influential role in the WTS environment; a group known by two separate designations: The Faithful & Discreet Slave and the Governing Body of Jehovah's Witnesses.

Persuasive Synonyms: The Faithful & Discreet Slave and the Governing Body

The first of these designations is The Faithful & Discreet Slave. I have chosen to capitalize this title based on the connotation of the name in the minds of devout JWs. Although such capitalization is never used in WTS literature, there is no doubt that for most JWs The Faithful & Discreet Slave represents a specific entity with a considerable amount of authority. The name derives from a passage in the New Testament, found at Matthew 24:45 in the *New World Translation* (Watch Tower, 2013a) wherein Jesus tells the story of a master who would appoint a "faithful and discreet slave" over all his servants. The slave appointed to this special position would be responsible for the well-being of all the other slaves including providing them "food at the proper time". The parallel account at Luke 12:42 employs a synonymic expression, "faithful steward" (Watch Tower, 2013a).

Jehovah's Witnesses have changed their theological understanding of The Faithful & Discreet Slave's identity over the decades. In the early Russellite movement, Russell himself was identified as the "faithful and discreet slave" referenced in Matthew 24:45, thus endowing him with prophetic significance. Later, WTS taught that a small minority of JWs who believe themselves to be chosen by God to be heavenly rulers (called "the anointed") made up an international, composite group that fulfilled Jesus' prophecy at Matthew 24:45 of a coming "faithful and discreet slave". This made for some rather confusing theology. Somehow, this group of elite JWs (comprising thousands of "anointed" JWs in disparate locations around the globe) was responsible for spiritual instruction and leadership in the "last days," and yet it was obvious that only those in leadership positions at world headquarters in New York had any authority special authority.

Further confusion came from a parallel doctrine asserting that a small group of anointed elders were responsible for the dissemination of doctrine and policy for the international brotherhood. This small board of leaders at headquarters in New York City was called the Governing Body.

The origin of the term Governing Body is explained well by George Chryssides in *Jehovah's Witnesses: Continuity and Change*. When referring to a non-canonical heading inserted into the organization's translation of Acts 15, he writes:

> Interestingly, one heading in the outline of Acts 15 reads "Letter from the governing body" referring to the apostles and elders who met at the First Council of Jerusalem. Although the term "governing body" does not appear in the translation itself, the Society clearly wishes to ensure that having a Governing Body was a feature

of the early Church (Chryssides, 2016, p. 168)

For years, confusion surrounded the relationship between "the faithful and discreet slave" of Matthew 24:45 and the Governing Body extrapolated from Acts 15. But the mystery was finally cleared up in a 2013 article in the *Watchtower* that succinctly identified "the faithful and discreet slave" as: "A small group of anointed brothers who are directly involved in preparing and dispensing spiritual food during Christ's presence. Today, these anointed brothers make up the Governing Body" (Watch Tower, 2013c).

Finally, it was clear: The Faithful & Discreet Slave is synonymous with the Governing Body. Most JWs appeared to be thankful for this unburdening of a complex doctrine. Now it was simple and powerful: the Governing Body is the "faithful and discreet slave" of Matthew 24:45. As a result, any mystical power and authority that devout JWs had attributed to The Faithful & Discreet Slave or the Governing Body was consolidated and arrogated by the eight-man board of spiritual leaders in Wallkill, New York.

Presently, the two terms, Governing Body and Faithful & Discreet Slave are used interchangeably by JWs to refer to their spirit-appointed leaders. As the *Watchtower* puts it:

> As a group, we willingly submit ourselves to the direction given by the Governing Body and cooperate with the appointed elders in the congregations. In such ways, we demonstrate our acceptance of God's way of ruling (…) Willing submission results in a worldwide unity that is

unique in this divided world. It also produces peace and righteousness and brings glory to Jehovah, demonstrating that his way of ruling is by far the best. (Watch Tower, 2010)

This "willing submission" forms the basis for compliance with the Governing Body. In earlier decades (before the explosion of information facilitated by the internet), less attention was given to the individual men on the Governing Body. It was not uncommon for even devout JWs to be unfamiliar with the Governing Body member's names. However in 2014, the rollout of JW Broadcasting, an internet streaming channel produced by WTS, brought greater attention to the eight men. In recent years, as a result of scriptural talks given by members of the Governing Body featured on JW Broadcasting regularly, it appears that personal devotion to the individual members of the Governing Body has increased.

Personal loyalty to the Governing Body strengthens as an individual takes on more theocratic responsibilities. For example, to become a volunteer in any official capacity with the non-profit organizations used by WTS (the Christian Congregation of Jehovah's Witnesses, the Religious Order of Jehovah's Witnesses), applicants must answer affirmatively to the question: "Do you believe that spiritual food from Jehovah is being provided through the faithful and discreet slave, and are you living in harmony with its teaching?" (Religious Order of Jehovah's Witnesses, 2015). An affirmative answer must be supported by acceptable answers to questions regarding an applicant's personal life including any history of mental health treatment or recent indulgences in sexually explicit music, pornography, or homosexuality.

Reference to the role of the Faithful & Discreet Slave or Governing Body is highly disproportionate to the appearance of these designations in biblical scripture. Nevertheless, obedience and submission to the direction of this body form a fundamental cognitive construct upon which rests the organization's environment of ideological totalism.

Lifton's Criteria of Ideological Totalism

The American psychiatrist and author Robert Jay Lifton researched the methods of a political reform movement sponsored by the Chinese communist party in the early 1950s that was designed to remold the thinking of Chinese citizens in acceptance of Marxism–Leninism and Maoism. The name of the program in Chinese is roughly translated: Thought Reform. Lifton described this program as "a systematic effort at political purification of individual minds" and "a quintessential example of ideological totalism." In Lifton's estimate, the program had been very successful and reaching its goal – altering the thinking of Chinese citizens and indoctrinating them in the party's ideology.

Lifton uses the term ideological totalism to refer to "an all-or-none set of ideas that claim nothing less than absolute truth and equally absolute virtue". Ideological totalism "suggests a system of ideas projected outward with the claim of providing solutions to all human problems." Offering a framework for the phenomenon, Lifton identifies "eight deadly sins" of ideological totalism; a list of eight sociological elements that can be used to identify ideologically totalist communities and that lead to the psychological phenomenon of thought reform.

Lifton writes in the introduction to the latest edition of his work: "I came to realize that ideological totalism and cultlike behavior not only blend with each other but tend to be part of a single entity" (Lifton, 2019, p.9). Ever since Lifton's *Thought Reform & The Psychology of Totalism* was published in 1961, the eight deadly sins have become a benchmark used by ex-members of high control groups to identify the psychological phenomenon they experienced.

In the following discussion, I will identify each of Lifton's eight criteria of ideological totalism and how I and many others experience them in the JW sub-culture.

1) Milieu Control

As the name implies, milieu control is the orchestration of one's social and informational environment. This includes not only the curation of a member's associates but also of all forms of communication, including the literature a person reads and the audio and video content they consume. Milieu control is essentially heavy-handed censorship of disapproved people and media.

Although JWs hold jobs and attend public schools, they still qualify as a closed community. In the early days of doctrinal acceptance, it is not uncommon for newly interested ones to distance themselves from non-believing family and friends. Gradually, a new Bible student focuses more and more of their emotional reliance on their new JW family. Of course, an individual's newly formed association with JWs usually raises the concern of family and friends. However, notice how their disapproval is reframed by WTS in the article "The Truth Brings, 'Not Peace, But a Sword'":

> Even when our relatives oppose our efforts to worship Jehovah, we continue to love them, but we must remember that our love for God and Christ comes first. (Matthew 10:37) We must also realize that Satan will try to use our affection for our family to break our integrity. (Watch Tower, 2017c)

The belief that affection for non-witness relatives can be exploited by the archnemesis of God motivates many members to further reduce the level of intimacy they have with non-witness family. Adherents are assured that, in the words of Christ, "no one has left house or brothers or sisters or mother or father or children or fields for my sake and for the sake of the good news who will not get a hundredfold now (…) and in the coming system of things everlasting life" (Mark 10:29,30; Watch Tower, 2013a). The same can be said of old friends.

The idea that media is an extension of one's social milieu, as Lifton also suggests, is addressed directly in WTS literature: "Association with those who do not adhere to God's laws— whether at school or at work or through some form of ungodly entertainment—might affect our determination to do what is right" (Watch Tower, 2009, p. 19).

The final psychological state created by milieu control, Lifton says, is personal closure; an individual who has been restricted from a thorough intellectual exploration of matters gives in to the pressure to polarize their thinking and accept the community's informational boundaries. Personal closure creates a childlike avoidance of the struggle to reconcile the "elusive subtleties of truth" (Lifton, 2019, p.31) and further psychological development is stymied.

2) Mystical Manipulation

According to Lifton, mystical manipulation is the creation of a supernatural aura around developments within a society or organization. Leaders of the movement assume the role of messengers of God chosen to direct the mission. The directives of leadership thus become superior in weight to all contradictory information and viewpoints. Additionally, rather than simply extolling the superiority of the group's beliefs, leadership will espouse the unnaturalness or ignorance of opposing viewpoints. Lifton explains that the psychological response to such mystical manipulation is a naive trust in every utterance proceeding from leadership, "like a child in the arms of its mother" (Lifton, 2019, p.31).

I remember an edition of JW Broadcasting that came out when I was experiencing the worst of my symptoms, entitled *In Whom Do You Trust?* The broadcast was appeared to be a response to recent accusations against the Governing Body by the media. Governing Body member Gerrit Lösch, after reminding viewers of the demonic influence upon the world at large, said:

Today the Faithful Slave was put in charge of providing spiritual food for God's people who number into the millions. The Slave also shows complete trust in Jehovah that he will guide them with his holy spirit. (…) Today Jehovah provides direction to the Slave through Jesus. Jesus, in turn, provides direction for his people through the Faithful and Discreet Slave. We can have, therefore, full confidence in their scriptural insight, understanding, and guidance. (Watch Tower, 2018c)

Comments like the above, attributing leadership to Christ and god's holy spirit, are usually interpreted as evidence of the humility of the Governing Body. Many JWs comment about how impressed they are impressed that such godly men resist the temptation to draw attention to their personal accomplishments. This is mystical manipulation at its finest.

Another example of mystical manipulation is WTS theology regarding the Bible writer, Ezekiel's vision of the celestial chariot. In the Bible book of Ezekiel, the author describes a quick-moving chariot ablaze and fitted with precious stones. JWs understand the celestial heavenly chariot to represent God's organization at its ability to move immediately in any direction at Jehovah's whim. Loyal JWs respond to doctrinal updates and policy changes with the trite exclamation: "The chariot is on the move!"

3) The Demand for Purity

It is the childlike mind that clings rigidly to the concepts of black and white, good and bad, right and wrong. As an individual matures psychologically across the lifespan, polarized black-and-white thinking bifurcates into myriad shades of gray. The result is that to the extent that humans develop psychologically and philosophically, they begin to recognize that no ideology can be considered completely pure and must base their decisions, not on rigid ideological doctrine, but on a kind of cost–benefit analysis performed against personally prescribed values. This modest reluctance of mature minds to avoid inflexible moral judgments is not a hallmark of the JW community.

Of course, JWs are quick to concede that leaders and laymen are prone to common human imperfection. The concept of forgivable imperfection, however, is equally flawed as it implies the existence of a standard of perfection to which one can measure their morality. So, while an individual JW is more than willing to admit her mistakes, she believes that her moral precepts issue from the Creator and are therefore wholly pure and righteous. Demand for purity rests on the assumption that an idyllic state of being exists, albeit nowhere else but in the spirit realm.

This isn't simply a matter of a community establishing high moral standards. Lifton highlights how this philosophical flaw has "more malignant consequences". He states that "by defining and manipulating the criteria of purity, and then by conducting an all-out war upon impurity, the ideological totalist creates a narrow world of guilt and shame" (Lifton, 2019, p.32).

As a result of this shame-ridden existence, members self-identify as flawed and sinful at the deepest psychological level. When JWs recognize in themselves errant thoughts or desires, or if they behave in a way contrary to the WTS code of conduct, they believe that they deserve a disciplinary response from congregation elders. As Lifton puts it, "one is expected to expect humiliation and ostracism" (Lifton, 2019, p.32). For many JWs, incessant feelings of guilt and shame can significantly contribute to long-term psychological conflict.

The doctrines of inherent sinfulness and redemption by God's grace are common in mainstream Christianity. It is a recipe for compulsive behavior and religious scrupulosity. But this effect is exacerbated in the case of JWs because of the strict control of the social milieu. JWs are never exposed to trusted voices that can moderate the intensity of religiously inspired shame. Perhaps my readers can imagine a situation wherein a conscientious child, prompted to self-hatred by one parent's religiosity, approaches his other more secularized and agnostic parent for a well-needed dilution of the faith-based guilt and some gentle reaffirmation: "It's not that big a deal. You're a good person." Believing JWs, with no outside voice of moderation and reason, have only God's mercy as administered by congregation elders to relieve such self-hatred.

But the real game of psychological ping-pong occurs when WTS literature suggests that ongoing feelings of worthlessness are evidence of a lack of faith in the atoning value of the ransom sacrifice of Christ. Now, the guilt-ridden JW begins not only to doubt their worth in the eyes of God but also the depth of their spirituality; their strength of belief in the very tenet of faith prescribed to resolve them of guilt. A feedback loop of guilt resonates with increasing force: guilt from an errant thought or action compounded by guilt over feeling guilty, about feeling guilty, over feeling guilty, about feeling guilty…

This pressure cooker of shame may lead to two negative psychological outcomes. One is the projection of internal conflict upon others, particularly upon a person who triggers awareness of an errant desire. The defensive individual turns to attack the human manifestation of their unspoken desire. This leads to further social alienation as members form bitter prejudices against people whose lifestyles remind them of the sacrifices they have made for their religious community.

The second result is the onset of depressive symptoms. Guilt and shame have long been associated with depression. Given the incessant reminders that JWs receive of their failure to live up to pure standards, depression is not surprising.

4) The Cult of Confession

Many readers will have experienced the catharsis, either therapeutically or by way of emotional vulnerability with a close friend or romantic partner, of confessing one's deepest, darkest secrets. To have a comrade with whom you can be your true self is one of the highlights of a close friendship. Loyalty based on trust in the confidentiality of shared vulnerabilities creates intimacy. However, it is also true that knowing another's vulnerabilities supplies one with a certain power to manipulate the weakness by threatening to reveal the secret. Secrets can be held as collateral over confessors. This dark reality is implicit in all trusting relationships.

In the totalist environment, however, a "purging milieu" exists wherein members compulsively confess to leadership and bestow upon them ownership of all their existential guilt. This leads to a social environment wherein leadership has complete access to all past transgressions and intimate knowledge of each member's tendencies toward thinking and behavior that transgress the organization's rules. Lifton states that this constant confession leads to a brotherhood of fellow sinners with whom all transgressions are shared and, eventually, "the dissolution of self into the great flow of the Movement" (Lifton, 2019, p.33).

No secrets, no self.

WTS encourages members to confess freely to elders whenever their conscience is troubled. As mentioned in the last chapter, this can result in unexpected disciplinary action. Further, elders document and maintain hard-copy reports of all judicial cases. They subsequently share information about confessions of all kinds with those above them in the hierarchy, including circuit overseers (traveling representatives of WTS headquarters) and headquarters staff themselves. The compulsion to confess is strong, as evidenced by one of my journal entries during my journey of recovery from Religious Trauma:

> 3/25/19
>
> I am choosing to dismiss the constant barrage in my mind that I am a filthy liar for not reporting my

sins. Holy hell, this is ridiculous. So stupid.

But it continues to feel so real. I am trying to reframe my brain to know that the Kingdom Hall is just the church I go to on Sundays; where my friends go, where my wife goes.

It's just a building I sit in a couple of times a week.

The emotional pull toward confessing my thought crime was intense.

Confessed sins also loom threateningly over the errant individual for months and years into the future. Appointments to oversight roles within the organization require a clean judicial record. Also, when JWs move geographically and start attending a new congregation, elders from the old congregation write a letter to the new congregation's elder body. This letter describes the spiritual history of the family and includes mention of past failings, even those of a non-judicial nature. The lay-witness is not privy to the details of such a letter, but most are aware that they do not enter the new congregation with a clean bill of health.

5) The "Sacred Science"

Lifton continues, "The totalist milieu maintains an aura of sacredness around its basic dogma, holding it out as an ultimate moral vision for the ordering of human existence." For JWs, the sacred science is WTS doctrine, considered to have emanated from the almighty creator of the universe. Further, Lifton states that "while transcending ordinary concerns of logic" ideologically totalist doctrine "makes an exaggerated claim at airtight logic" (Lifton, 2019, p.34). WTS theology describes the Bible as a flawless guide for philosophical truth and morality. Elaborate defenses are published in WTS literature and memorized by JWs in preparation for encounters in the door-to-door proselytizing work. Baptism requires an in-depth study of this complex theology, chronology, and prophecy.

JWs see the body of truth as an ever-evolving "sacred secret" described as "an aspect of God's purpose that originates with God, is withheld until his own time, and is revealed only to those whom he chooses to make it known" (Watchtower, 2013a) According to JW doctrine, the "sacred secret" was gradually divulged through the pages of the Bible and throughout the history of God's people by means of a series of covenants between Jehovah and his chosen people. Each covenant gradually shed more light on God's overarching purpose. It is only in the last days (that is, post-1914) that the true knowledge of God has become abundant as a result of WTS's evangelization efforts (Watch Tower, 2012c)

All scriptural teachings are said to fall within the "standard of wholesome words" (2 Timothy 1:13, Watch Tower, 2013a). Bible principles can thus be used as a formula of sorts to determine the correct behavioral response to every situation. For many devout JWs, this scriptural arithmetic has the appearance of a grand and multifaceted architecture of divine governance.

Thus, when shown to be satisfactorily based on biblical principles, every directive issuing from the organization is interpreted as an extension of the sacred science, as a logical extrapolation of mutually accepted doctrine. This contributes to the thinking among the devout that criticism of any policy, be it organizational or logistic, is evidence of spiritual weakness.

6) Loading the Language

Language can open the mind to new ways of thinking. Creative expression sends cognition in new directions that at once ignite new connections and insights. As linguist Noam Chomsky puts it in *What Kind of Creatures Are We?*, language is primarily a function of the mind even before that of the tongue. The brain's aptitude for creating infinitely expression with a limited set of linguistic tools is the basis for an ever-expanding memeplex and subsequent delivery of new ideas into human consciousness, whether spoken or in written form.

Conversely, the repetitive use of language constricts thought and is indicative of ideologically totalist societies. Lifton calls the oft-repeated expressions of totalist environments "thought-terminating clichés". He describes such terms this way: "The most far-reaching and complex of human problems are compressed into brief, highly reductive, definitive-sounding phrases, easily memorized and easily expressed" (Lifton, 2019, p.34).

Lifton's comments dovetail with Chomsky's. Just as infinite possibilities in the construction of linguistic cognition can yield creative outputs, so limited and reductive language has the effect of stymieing thought: "One is, so to speak, linguistically deprived; and since language is so central to all human experience, one's capacity for thinking and feeling are immensely narrowed" (Lifton, 2019, p.35).

It is not difficult to notice such language in conversations with JWs. One might chalk it up to a general lack of education; research from Pew in 2016 found that sixty-three percent of JWs in the US do not have a college education (Lipka, 2016). But the restricted use of language is more critical than that. "Thought-terminating clichés" are used when conversations diverge into a territory that allows for disunifying opinion or natural human emotion that might challenge the sacred science and accepted community norms.

The following is a list of such terms and how they support the psychological captivity of JWs by arresting dissenting thought:

> "That's why we need God's kingdom"—When JWs talk about world events, they do so as third-party observers. At times, they can display a cold aloofness to human suffering. The burdens of democratic responsibility for social progress do not weigh heavily on the mind of a devout JW. When conversations about injustice in the world become difficult or point in the direction of community responsibility, JWs shy away from obligation and await God's kingdom. "That's why we need God's kingdom" serves to block further temptation to involve oneself in the humanitarian goals of the greater community.

> "As long as you are faithful to Jehovah"—I found

this thought-terminating cliché to be particularly painful as I was stepping down from some higher profile responsibilities in the organization. When a JW makes a lifestyle choice that is not overtly recommended by the organization (but is still considered allowable) "as long as you are faithful to Jehovah" is a reminder of the firm line in the sand. In other words: you are pushing the envelope, but if you leave the organization, that is the end of our relationship.

"Leave it in Jehovah's hands"—This is, of course, not unique to JWs. When expressions in mainstream Christianity like "hand it to Jesus" are employed too often, they can induce mental sloth and stunt pragmatic problem-solving.

"The chariot is on the move"—I mentioned this one earlier. When changes to congregation procedure or theology trickle down from WTS headquarters, any criticism of the change or questioning of the motives of leadership is likely to be terminated with this reference to God's heavenly government. The comment implies that there is no need for the JW to analyze the rationale for the adjustment at length. The decision came straight from the heavens. Move on and pretend that the change is the greatest thing that has ever happened to you. Thank Jehovah for it in your private prayers.

I could go on. Many Bible passages themselves qualify as thought-terminating clichés. And all JWs share the same interpretation of Bible verses and their application to everyday conduct. Drop a Bible quote during a philosophical debate, and the conversation ends. So does dissenting thought.

7) Doctrine over Person

Lifton describes "doctrine over person" as the power that a collective myth has to rewrite history and personal interpretation of experience. "Rather than modify the myth in accordance with experience, the will to orthodoxy requires that men be modified in order to reaffirm the myth" (Lifton, 2019, p.35).

So, when personal experience does not line up with the worldview prescribed by WTS, JWs reinterpret their personal experience. This can require some rather creative rationalization. For example, if one receives a job offer that conflicts with congregation meetings, it may be interpreted as a temptation from the Devil. Conversely, a job that allows for part-time work and part-time preaching is a gift from Jehovah—until the boss of that accommodating job demands that you work on Sunday morning at the same time as the congregation meeting. Then, maybe that job was not from God after all. Similarly, when governments imprison JWs for refusal of military service, it may be claimed that Satan is influencing them. But when the authorities release incarcerated JWs for humanitarian reasons, governments are said to be powerless to Jehovah's will.

The constant reinterpretation of personal intuition may create a distinct lack of trust in the self and a diminished ability to make assertive life decisions. Perhaps more pervasively, aligning one's personal life experiences with the complex JW theology applies cosmic significance to the most mundane personal and interpersonal experiences. Thus, the wholescale faith dissolution that occurs when a JW awakens can cast all their life experiences into question, taint them with betrayal and pain, and leave the individual feeling as if their most cherished life experiences cannot be leveraged as a source of objective experiential evidence.

8) The Dispensing of Existence

In this final criterion, the predisposition for in-group loyalty and out-group hostility is sanctified in official doctrine. "The totalist environment draws a sharp line between those whose right to existence can be recognized, and those who possess no such right" (Lifton, 2019, p.36). Non-witnesses are referred to as "worldly," not in the secular sense of the word but in the sense of James 4:4, which states that whoever "wants to be a friend of the world is constituting himself an enemy of God."

It could be said that JWs present a much different face to outsiders than they do to active members. In *Jehovah's Witnesses: Continuity and Change*, George Chryssides, who evidently spent much time with a local congregation as a visiting outsider, firmly states that he was never treated any differently because he was not an official member of the congregation. He explains that he never got the impression that JWs altered their behavior for his benefit to "present themselves in a more favorable light" (Chryssides, 2016, p.21). Let me tell you, George, I've been a full-time evangelizer struggling to fulfill my required seventy-plus hours of proselytizing each month. If I had so much as gone to tea with you, I would have had my game face on, and reported the time on my monthly field service report.

Dispensing of existence also happens at disfellowshipping when the chairman announces: "Such and such is no longer one of Jehovah's Witnesses." When outsiders call JWs a cult, blame them for killing babies, or other such extreme speech, JWs rally in support of each other and put up a fierce defense. But this defense is even more impressive when someone with inside knowledge of the community expresses a critical view to outsiders. Ex-members who repeatedly criticize the religion are labeled as apostates and disfellowshipped. In JW psychology, the term apostate goes beyond the common connotation. This is evidenced by the use of the definite article when referring to these enemies of the truth as "the apostates." Until I effectively became one, I too imagined "the apostates" to be a particularly evil group of ex-JWs with centralized governance similar to WTS itself. Becoming an apostate is worse than death, worse even than being disfellowshipped. It carries the connotation of malicious belligerence against Jehovah's chosen people and outright persecution of the brotherhood.

Additionally, apostates are considered as slippery as the serpent in Eden—deceitful and manipulative. Notice how *Watchtower* dispenses of their opponents' existence:

> Their methods reveal a cunning spirit. Apostates "quietly bring in" corruptive ideas. Like smugglers, they operate in a clandestine manner, subtly

introducing apostate views. And just as a clever forger tries to pass phony documents, so apostates use "counterfeit words," or false arguments, trying to pass their fabricated views as if they were true. (Watch Tower, 2011b)

This book too will no doubt be labeled as the scheming work of a sinister apostate.

As have many others, I found Lifton's framework to be particularly beneficial as I made sense of what had happened to me during my time as a passionately devout JW. Call it what you will, but there is a distinct sociopsychological air when you enter the door of a closed religious community intent on gathering more followers to the cause. The unsuspecting can easily be swept up and eventually, lose their semblance of self in the collective consciousness of movement. Children raised in such an environment are hardly aware that there is any other way to think.

That is until the veil of religious piety lifts. As I will discuss in chapter 5, the process of awakening is no less than traumatic.

4. A Crisis of Conscience: Ethical Implications

In the spring of 2017, I was in the throes of some of the worst symptoms associated with Religious Trauma Syndrome. Panic attacks were a regular occurrence. These came mostly as a result of what I considered at the time to be blasphemous thoughts that repeated uncontrollably in my mind: irrepressible rebelliousness and anger against the Almighty Creator of the Universe. My mind searched for relief from my psychological conflict in thoughts of death. Flashes in consciousness of my wrists slit and bleeding over the edge of a bathtub punished me on an hourly basis. Suicidal ideation led to compulsive prayer; begging God for relief with the obsessive furiousness and redundancy of an obsessive-compulsive disorder (OCD) patient flipping a light switch on the way out of the house.

Still, I could not put my finger on the problem. No matter how hard I prayed, how often I read the Bible, how much WTS material I studied, I was overcome by unwanted thoughts of disbelief and the nagging message of my subconscious mind, telling me I could no longer support the mission of WTS as I had in the past. These were no longer the religious doubts that I had grown accustomed to growing up as a zealous JW observing the world around me from an aloof distance. As hard as I tried, I could no longer hold the doctrinal arguments together. The fabric of "the truth" was unraveling.

A search of my symptoms on the *Watchtower Library*

CD-ROM, the only organizationally sanctioned tool for research material untainted by Satanic influence, shed no new spiritual light on my situation. That is to say, other than what I already knew: there is no place in Jehovah's organization for a spirit of rebelliousness.

> Many persons outside Jehovah's organization today exercise what they term "complete freedom" of thought and action. They adopt a philosophy that allows them to satisfy their every whim. Because they do not wish to be restricted in any sense, they refuse to accept the pure Word of God as a guide, and they continue on their course of self-styled freedom. This is a rebellious course and is causing those who practice this to be fit only for destruction at the battle of Armageddon (Watch Tower, 1958, p.219).

My unwelcome intrusive thoughts of rebellion against my religious community rendered me "fit for destruction." I found no relief in the Bible or the material published by WTS.

I tried to use my best secular vocabulary to explain the situation to my general practitioner doctor. I told him I was having "some kind of crisis of faith." He, in modesty (or perhaps cowardice), deflected. He refused to broach the possibility that my faith was causing my mental illness.

It was one night in the small hours of the morning, alone with my anxieties and the intrusive thoughts of a subconscious that refused to obey the regulation of my ego, that my mind alighted on an expression: I was having a crisis of conscience. The expression seemed to fit exactly what I was experiencing. I could not figure out whether I considered it ethically right or wrong to continue supporting WTS. I could not figure out what the "right" thing to do was. Or rather, all available options seemed to have elements of rightness and wrongness such that an unequivocally appropriate course of action was impossible to identify.

Given the limited vocabulary of my community and upbringing, I had never before considered the crisis of conscience as a moral concept. I Googled the term. To my horror, the first result from Wikipedia stated: "*Crisis of Conscience* is a biographical book by Raymond Franz, a former member of the Governing Body of Jehovah's Witnesses, written in 1983, three years after his expulsion from the Jehovah's Witnesses denomination."

I slammed the laptop down with a mixture of terror and what was left of my righteous indignation.

I was becoming an apostate after all.

An Ethical Dilemma

As mentioned at the outset, the purpose of this volume is not to present an overall critique of JW beliefs. It is not my intent to analyze the accuracy of WTS doctrine in comparison to the collection of Hebrew, Aramaic, and Greet sacred texts known as the Holy Bible. And I am not interested in proclaiming that it is "wrong" or "right," "good" or "evil" to be a JW. Such polarized thinking is a cognitive distortion. That kind of thinking was at the root of my psychological trauma and is diametrically opposed to the purpose of *A Voice from Inside*. However, a few critical WTS beliefs and policies have grave ethical consequences and thus bear upon the thesis of this volume, as I will show.

Many JWs find their lifestyle rewarding and fulfilling. They enjoy the comradery of the brotherhood. They share good times with friends and family. They fulfill their obligations within the congregation and in their door-to-door ministry to the extent that they are comfortable. The high demand of their religious community is just part of their culture and feels sustainable.

This is not dissimilar to how many modern churchgoers pick and choose the parts of their doctrine that they find personally comforting or motivating and dismiss those that seem absurd or unnecessary. So too with JWs. Individual members vary in their propensity for spirituality and the amount of time and effort that they commit to supporting the WTS mission.

But when a religious belief or policy has the potential to cause significant harm to others, whether they are active members or outsiders, doctrine must be put under ethical scrutiny. Because of the captive environment, totalist ideology, and enforced all-or-nothing support of doctrinal implementation in day-to-day life, the ethically questionable aspects of WTS theology are amplified and create a real dilemma: To what extent should the free exercise of religious belief be allowed to cause harm to others?

For most JWs, this is not a problem at all. Their firm belief in the Bible and God's selection of the Watch Tower Bible & Tract Society of Pennsylvania as the one true religion allows them to abdicate responsibility for any ethical violations proliferated by the organization's teachings.

However, when the overarching belief in God, the Bible, and the Faithful & Discreet Slave is no longer sustainable, as is the case to varying degrees with PIMOs, the belief system's potential for considerable harm is brought into glaring focus. This is particularly relevant for those who were heavily involved in proselytizing or administering WTS policy. For example, PIMOs who were pioneers and missionaries may have converted others to the faith by way of one-on-one in-home Bible studies that eventually led to formal dedication and baptism. And PIMOs who were elders before disillusionment were complicit in enforcing policies of coercion upon new and existing members.

Ethical dilemmas are at the heart of RTS. The comorbidity of RTS and a subset of PTSD called moral injury, associated with the violation of personal moral principles, will be analyzed in Chapter 6. For now, let us discuss some of the ethical issues that appear most often in internet posts from ex-members as reasons for guilt and remorse over their actions while they were practicing JWs.

Violations of Religious Freedom

JWs consider themselves experts in the subject of religious freedom. Because of their separateness and a belief system that is occasionally perceived as threatening to some political parties, Jehovah's Witnesses have fought considerable legal battles for the right to freely practice their religion. Indeed, they have been credited for their contributions to the protection of religious freedom in both the United States and the European Court of Human Rights (ECHR). Some landmark cases have benefitted the larger community by regulating the power of federal governments to encroach upon the basic human freedom to practice one's beliefs. For example, in the US Supreme Court case *Minersville School District v. Gobitis* in 1940, JWs won the right for their children to abstain from saluting the American flag at the beginning of each school day. Religious minorities and dissenting political groups can be thankful to WTS for this freedom.

There is a group, however, whose freedom to practice their religion or to object to the practicing of a certain religion is supported neither by the United States Supreme Court nor the ECHR nor WTS. It is the right of the disillusioned Jehovah's Witness to worship freely according to their personal spiritual convictions. "They are free to leave," many would say. But the reality is that harmony with one's family is often a central tenet of a belief system and a sacred value of the non-religious spiritual seeker. For the atheist and the agnostic, spiritual values are often self-constructed. They may base their values on knowledge acquired from the scientific domains of physics and biology, and the softer sciences of the humanities. If a PIMO is ethically opposed to the mission or policies of WTS, but holds to a religious or spiritual value of unity with their biological family or other social supports, the captive policies of disfellowshipping, disassociation, and enforced shunning of WTS prohibits a PIMO's free expression of their beliefs.

Outside of the fully disillusioned PIMO, who may be agnostic or atheist, there are other subsets of JWs whose religious rights are restricted. Although the polarizing nature of the rhetoric often forces fading members to make an overt all-in or all-out decision, a small minority of members exist who believe in the WTS as an agent of God's use but who disagree with a particular belief or behavioral injunction of the organization. Though these individuals may choose to support the work of the organization, their dissenting voice is largely silenced, and they are restricted from living in a way that is in harmony with their spiritual values when it brings them into conflict with official organization theology or policy. In the realms of sexual expression, interfaith activity, health care choices, or political affiliation, members are not permitted to openly practice their self-prescribed belief systems.

The challenge of placing limits on freedoms affects all organized institutions. True freedom is an ideological illusion and any integration of an individual with a community requires some restriction of their freedoms for the sake of the functioning of the group. Leaders must decide how to address issues where the beliefs of one member conflict with the free expression of another. In other cases, policymakers must adjudicate when the right to one freedom has the potential to encroach upon another. It is their responsibility to decide how to protect such freedoms for the greatest number possible.

In the proceedings of the Australian Royal Commission mentioned in the introduction, Angus Stewart's examination of the Governing Body member Geoffrey Jackson addresses the contradiction in JW belief regarding freedom of religion. The below (Royal Commission, 2015) is in the context of a discussion about the restrictions on the religious freedoms of victims of sexual abuse within the congregation. If an abuser is deemed repentant by the elders, he or she will be allowed to remain in the organization. Simultaneously, the victim cannot leave the organization if they desire to maintain the familial and social relationships that provide support in the wake of incredible trauma.

> Stewart: Does the Jehovah's Witness organization then recognize an individual's freedom to make religious choices?

> Jackson: Yes, we do.

> (…)

> Stewart: And, Mr. Jackson, you have put it that they have a choice to leave or not to leave. For someone who wants to leave, perhaps because they have suffered abuse by someone in the organization and don't feel that it has been treated properly or adequately, it's a very difficult choice, isn't it, because they must choose.

> Jackson: I agree, yes.

> Stewart: And it can be a very cruel choice for

them—not so?

Jackson: I agree, it's a difficult choice.

Stewart: And it can be personally devastating because they can lose their whole social network and their families?

Jackson: That can be the case, yes.

Stewart: Would you accept, then, that putting people to that choice, through this system of disassociating from them or shunning, as it is sometimes referred to, is contrary to the Jehovah's Witness belief in freedom of religious choice?

Jackson: No, I don't accept that. I think you are jumping to a conclusion there, but I understand that you have that opinion.

(…)

Stewart: You see, let's take someone who is baptized at a young age and then, as a young adult, decides that actually their beliefs lie elsewhere, and they want to choose some other system of belief. They then are still going to be faced with the stark choice that we have identified, aren't they?

Jackson: That's true.

Stewart: And it's on that basis, I suggest to you, that the policy and practice of the organization is in conflict with the Jehovah's Witnesses' belief, as you have said it is, in freedom of religious choice?

Jackson: No, we don't see it that way, but you are entitled to your opinion.

PIMOs are entitled to their opinions, but not their religious freedom.

Blood

I approach discussing the ethics of the JW blood doctrine with caution. As is the case of all recommendations related to the physiological health of the human organism, nonprofessionals must be modest in their assertions. Frankly, we do not live in an era of modesty in this respect. From veganism to ketosis and vaccines to homeopathic remedies, discussion of recent scientific findings by both the journalist and the layperson quickly become polarized. This is usually because of the limited expertise of the interlocutors.

WTS presents a compelling case for the superior quality of bloodless medicine for many complex medical procedures. Indeed, there is much academic literature surrounding the use of such non-blood medicine. And the ethically informed community of medical practitioners is eager to cooperate with the religious beliefs of their JW patients. This has led to increases in bloodless technology and improved outcomes for JWs in general. However, I cannot agree with George Chryssides' categorical statement in *Jehovah's Witnesses: Continuity and Change*: that "if a blood transfusion is advised, Jehovah's Witnesses are not faced with the stark alternatives of apostasy or death" (Chryssides, 2016, p.192). While they may not *necessarily* be subject to this dichotomy, current WTS policy and doctrine may cause this eventuality in some cases.

From *Shepherd the Flock of God:*

> If someone willingly accepts a blood transfusion, perhaps because of being under extreme pressure, a committee (not judicial) should obtain the facts and determine the individual's attitude. If he is repentant, the committee would provide spiritual assistance in the spirit of Galatians 6:1 and Jude 22, 23. Since he is spiritually weak, he would not qualify for special privileges for a period of time. In some cases, it may also be necessary to remove other privileges, such as commenting at congregation meetings and presenting student assignments on the midweek meeting. Depending on the circumstances, the committee may also need to arrange for an announcement to the congregation at a midweek meeting: "The elders have handled a matter having to do with [name of person]. You will be glad to know that spiritual shepherds are endeavoring to render assistance." On the other hand, if the elders on the committee determine that he is unrepentant, they should announce his disassociation. (Watch Tower, 2019a)

Once again, there is no middle ground. Either one refuses blood, or they are not one of Jehovah's Witnesses and are subject to shunning by their entire social support system, including their immediate family.

WTS theology prohibits the acceptance of lifesaving transfusion of whole blood or the four main components of blood: plasma, red blood cells, white blood cells, and platelets. To the extent that lives are lost from the refusal of blood and blood components in medical treatment, those who persuade members to obey the blood doctrine and could be considered ethically culpable.

The question is not about the efficacy of bloodless medicine, but whether JWs are acting "autonomously and uniformly in refusing blood," a question posed by Osamu Muramoto in a three-part series in the *Journal of Medical Ethics* from 1998 to 2000. Muramoto shows how the policies of disfellowshipping and disassociation combined with the atmosphere of self-policing in the JW community coerce patients into conforming to the JW policy of refusing blood transfusions. (Muramoto, 1998). Muramoto quotes from the September 1st, 1987 *Watchtower* which presents this scenario:

> One day Mary faced a dilemma. In processing medical records, she came upon information indicating that a patient, a fellow Christian, had submitted to an abortion. Did she have a Scriptural responsibility to expose this information to elders in the congregation, even though it might lead to her losing her job, to her being sued, or to her employer's having legal problems?

Watchtower provides a clear answer:

> Mary was somewhat apprehensive about the legal aspects but felt that in this situation Bible principles should carry more weight than the requirement that she protect the privacy of the medical records. (…) So when Mary analyzed all the facts available to her, she decided conscientiously that this was a time to "speak," not to "keep quiet." (Watch Tower, 1987)

In the conclusion of his discussion, Muramoto draws attention to WTS's censorship of medical and ethical points of view from outsiders. He states, "the coercion in the JW community not to review and examine critical information is both covert and overt" (Muramoto, 1998, p.228).

Further, WTS sponsors Hospital Liaison Committees (HLC), a network of JW elders organized to support JW patients and their physicians as they navigate treatment decisions. However, because the HLC is made up of congregation elders—the same body that represents the executive branch of the organization's disciplinary policies—the HLC could be considered an extension of coercive policy to the hospital bedside itself. While many devout JWs seem to appreciate the support of these brothers in critical moments at the hospital, the fact remains that the only source of contrasting information or opinion regarding the lifesaving use of blood is from distrusted outsiders.

Even medical professionals, if not baptized witnesses, are considered by the rank and file to be part of Satan's system of things manipulated by him to make them compromise their faith. Indeed, the No Blood

Medical Directive that all baptized JWs carry in their wallets has become a sort of totem of loyalty to the brotherhood. It appears that the refusal of blood has become a subconscious martyrdom pact that unites the brotherhood at the utmost levels of spiritual intensity.

Given the life-threatening seriousness of the blood doctrine, WTS takes every precaution to ensure that JWs are well prepared for medical complications that may require the use of blood. Newly baptized members receive a packet of information about how to prepare themselves for such medical emergencies. Additionally, the secretary of all bodies of elders is tasked with providing information to any newly pregnant woman in the congregation about how to prepare for complications of childbirth that might necessitate a blood transfusion. Such provisions could be interpreted as pastoral concern if it weren't for the proactive muscling out of dissenting voices at every juncture. As the official website of the organization of PIMOs and ex-witnesses called *Advocates for Jehovah's Witness Reform on Blood* puts it:

> The patient may not have a clear understanding of what they are accepting or rejecting, and the lack of good alternatives. They may overestimate the effectiveness of blood transfusion alternatives, or lack clarity on logistical and spiritual permissibility of advance donation of their own blood, or blood fractions. There may be earnest or paternalistic clouding of this information by the JW Hospital Liaison Committee (HLC). (Zieman, 2018)

It is in this self-policing and suppression of critical

information that, to a degree, all devout JWs are complicit. But as mentioned earlier, the extent of one's involvement influences the gravity of their culpability. Full-time proselytizers (called Regular Pioneers) handhold their spiritual protégés as they progress to baptism and beyond, elders teach the blood doctrine from the platform and enforce disciplinary policy, and parents convince their children that rejecting lifesaving treatment pleases their creator. Self-policing occurs at all strata of the hierarchy.

For the JW parent who grows disillusioned with the faith that their child died to uphold, reckoning with their complicity in the child's untimely death would likely be so traumatic that the parent's psychological defenses would simply never allow it. No doubt, similar psychological defense mechanisms prohibit Governing Body members from objectively reckoning with their contribution to the countless lives lost because of the blood doctrine.

Homophobia and Sexual Repression

An excellent analysis of the challenges of gay and lesbian JWs came out of the Department of Sociology of California State University of Chico, California. The authors, Janja Lalich, Ph.D., and Karla McLaren, provide an analysis of a subset of gay and lesbian JWs who chronicled their process of sexual self-realization on the internet. Lalich and McLaren explain how the challenges of coming out for an adolescent questioning their sexuality can be particularly complex for those who have a strong connection to their identity within a religious culture that condemns homosexual behavior (Lalich & McLaren, 2010).

While Christian religions tend to take varying approaches to harmonizing homosexuality with traditional doctrine, WTS theology does not allow for this moderation. WTS literature often compares the plight of the homosexual JW with that of an unmarried heterosexual who must exercise self-control so as not to engage in sexual conduct outside the biblically condoned use of sexual organs—namely, vaginal penetration between a married husband and wife. (Masturbation is considered a sin for the married or unmarried person. And oral and anal sex between a husband and wife is also discouraged.)

According to *Insight on the Scriptures*, the quintessential research manual of Jehovah's Witnesses, homosexuals "change the natural use of themselves into one contrary to nature" (Romans 1:26; Watch Tower, 2013a). Arguing for the unnaturalness of homosexuality even before it was formally and explicitly condemned in the Mosaic law and recorded in the Bible books of Leviticus and Deuteronomy, *Insight* says:

> Even though no specific law had been given, such a practice was *obviously* contrary to the way of God the Creator, as the very structure of the male and female manifested. Man, having been originally made in God's image, had intelligence sufficient to see these things. Hence, he was responsible before God if he went contrary to God's way; he was sinning, "missing the mark" even without a specifically stated law to charge him with guilt

[italics mine] (Watch Tower, 2018b, p. 223)

Based on the above, the homosexual JW is made to feel not only spiritually impure because of thoughts alone, but also unintelligent because they cannot comprehend the "obvious" unnaturalness of their desires. As Lalich & McLaren put it, "a homosexual Witness (including those who may be questioning their sexuality) must suppress both sexual behavior *and* sexual feelings" (Lalich & McLaren, 2010, p.1304).

Consider too the direction provided to elders regarding disciplinary action for congregation members who view pornography. While not all types of pornographic content are deemed of equal depravity, instructions are provided to determine whether a publisher's pornography use requires the formation of a judicial committee. In determining whether the pornography viewed should be considered "abhorrent" or not, *Shepherd the Flock of God* states:

> Such abhorrent forms of pornography include homosexuality (sex between those of the same gender (…) It is equally wrong for a man or woman to watch two women engaged in homosexual activity as it is for a man or woman to watch two men engaged in homosexual activity. (Watchtower, 2019a)

Despite the recent articles in *Watchtower* that attempt a more empathetic approach to the plight of JWs who battle inner desires for romantic and sexual relationships with the same sex, the fact remains that the rhetoric and attitude of organizational leadership and the community at large frame homosexuality as a graver sin than other forms of extramarital heterosexual expression. Homosexuality is considered abhorrent.

Of course, WTS is quick to give a solution to the homosexual's struggle: prayer, Bible reading, meditation. A publication designed specifically for adolescents in the organization, *Questions Young People Ask—Answers That Work, Volume 2*, offers this encouragement:

> Of course, some claim (…) that you should simply "embrace your sexuality" and "accept who you are." But the Bible says that you can do better than that! It tells us, for example, that some early Christians who had formerly practiced homosexuality *changed.* (1 Corinthians 6:9–11) You too can win the battle—even if at this point it's only being waged in your heart. (Watch Tower, 2012a)

And so, the homosexual Jehovah's Witness goes about the private psychological task of forcibly denying the genuine sexual self. This state has the potential to create compulsive thinking and behaviors. The process goes something like this: A homosexual thought arises in consciousness. A conditioned physiological fear response occurs following the realization that one has failed again to live up to God's standards, followed by self-loathing. And finally, the individual turns to compulsive prayers of confession, repentance, and a promise to try harder next time. As Lalich & McLaren put it, "This puts an enormous psychological burden on gay and lesbian JWs, as the control and elimination of thoughts and feelings becomes a near-impossible task" (Lalich & McLaren, 2010, p.1311). This psychological burden can lead to intrusive thoughts, depression, self-hatred, and low self-esteem.

It is hard to underestimate the psychological tension that results from forcibly denying the true self. Sexuality expression issues from the deepest realms of the human spirit. Gender identity and sexual orientation are tethered to the core of an individual's identity. And yet for many JWs, their identity is equally connected to their love for Jehovah. At their deepest self, they love Jehovah and their brotherhood.

But there is no middle road. They cannot be gay and one of Jehovah's Witnesses.

Dan Reynolds, lead singer of the alternative rock band Imagine Dragons, shed light on a similar struggle among LGBTQ+ youth in the Mormon community in his documentary film *Believer*, which addresses the increasing rate of suicide among Utah teenagers over the past few decades. In a moving scene that speaks to the heart of this identity conflict, Reynolds, who still identifies as a Mormon, and Neon Trees frontman Tyler Glenn, who was raised Mormon but later excommunicated for homosexuality, prepare for a concert to increase awareness of LGBTQ+ Mormons. While walking the grounds of the intended site of the concert three blocks away from the Mormon temple in Salt Lake City, they share a moment of spiritual unity and begin singing one of the Mormon hymns that they remember from their youth:

As I have loved you, love one another.

This new commandment; love one another

By this shall men know ye are my disciples

If ye have love, one to another

But Christ's love, as is that of so many of his followers, *is* conditional.

While psychological struggle is especially intense for LGBTQ+ JWs, shame and self-loathing based on sexual repression extend to others too. Given the organization's stance on the sinfulness of masturbation, a similar cognitive war on normal sexual desire can also cause unnecessary tension for heterosexuals in the organization. The book *Keep Yourself in God's Love*, published by WTS, states unequivocally, "A spiritually unhealthy habit, masturbation instills attitudes that foster self-centeredness and corrupt the mind" (Watch Tower, 2014a, p.218).

Another striking example comes from an orientation video for new entrants into WTS headquarters and branch offices. In the video, leaked online and subsequently named "Pillowgate" by prominent ex-JW YouTuber Lloyd Evans, responsible men in the organization instruct the new volunteers with the following:

> Suppose a brother starts rubbing his genitals against a pillow. He gets an erection but stops before having an orgasm. Is he masturbating? Yes again, because he is deliberately stimulating himself whether he has

an orgasm or not (…) How about having an emission of semen at night, maybe even after having an erotic dream? (…) When this happens to you, it would be good to examine whether you were dwelling on sexual thoughts before going to sleep. Could you have been sleeping in a position that stimulated you such as with a pillow or blanket held tightly between your legs? If you are honest with yourself about these matters, it will help you to avoid falling into unclean practices.

The video would be comical if it were not for the psychological implications of this intrusion of headquarters oversight into the private sexuality of its members. Such perverse views about human sexuality linger in the subconscious mind of the JWs and feed a vicious cycle of shame, self-hatred, and religious compulsion. For any who are genetically predisposed to neuroticism, this stress could very well be an ongoing source of depression and cause overwhelming feelings of worthlessness.

Restrictions Upon Self-Actualization

Establishing linkage between the cognitive infrastructures of religious belief and indicators of mental health is fraught with confounding factors. Seeking truth and discovering cognitive systems that contribute to mental well-being is the overarching spiritual journey of the *Homo sapiens*. The challenges of this quest can hardly be localized to one religious group. However overwhelming the task, this spiritual quest and the associated mitigation of religious extremism among humankind is of utmost importance. It is worthy work. Of course, none of us are going to get it right. To put it tritely, it's about the journey, not the destination. But along the way, we fine-tune our philosophies and share our insights with others to their benefit.

An ethical challenge occurs for the PIMO if they no longer believe that the framework of WTS beliefs is beneficial to the mental well-being of others. They may no longer believe that adherence to WTS statutes will afford them everlasting life. They might be disenthralled by the promised unity of an earthly brotherhood. In short, they no longer believe that the benefits of JW theology outweigh the disadvantages of belonging to the group. To the extent that they are compelled to maintain membership in the community and continue in the evangelical work as a WTS apologist, they will experience ethical conflict.

This is meaningful from a psychological perspective. Psychologists understand that not all belief systems are created equal. Distorted cognition leads to psychological distress. Left untreated, psychological distress leads to mental illness in the form of depression and anxiety. Cognitive distortions include black-and-white thinking, "should" statements, emotional reasoning, always being right, and the heaven's reward fallacy (the false belief that acts of self-denial are tallied up by an invisible force to be repaid at some undisclosed time in the future). Psychotherapists assist their clients to identify and challenge their distorted thinking with the goal of attaining a more balanced mental state. The space in this volume does not allow for a complete mapping of the scientifically established cognitive distortions to WTS doctrine. But a cursory examination has led many to draw such connections. The constant exposure of members within NRMs and HDRGs to cognitive distortions may make the treatment of mental illness even more problematic.

A common challenge of psychological research is the matter of correlation and causation. Does being in an HDRG *cause* mental illness or are individuals with a biological predisposition to mental illness attracted to the sociology or ideology of the group? To answer this question, researchers must control for confounding factors. I, therefore, cannot support with any evidence-based research statements to the effect that "being a Jehovah's Witness causes mental illness" or even that "Jehovah's Witnesses have a high level of mental illness." It will be the role of research psychologists to determine the connection between faith systems that enshrine cognitive distortions and mental ill-health. This is a touchy subject. But if humankind is going to protect itself against a repetition of the historical ills of religion, this work must be done.

My argument as it relates to this section is of the moral conundrum that a PIMO may face. A PIMO may choose to allow personal infractions upon their freedoms of expression in exchange for continued association with family members and friends. They may have resigned themselves to that sacrifice. However, a PIMO will experience distress when pressured to proliferate or identify with doctrine that she feels is not conducive to the spiritual or psychological well-being of others.

Personally, I am concerned for the mental health of

my fellow JWs. It is common knowledge that stressful environments can exacerbate mental illness. Growing up as a JW, I experienced considerable depression and anxiety punctuated by phases of intense guilt and self-loathing over my violations of the JW moral code. Only with the deconstruction of my faith have I been able to see significant improvement in my symptoms of depression and anxiety. Despite my ongoing association with JWs, liberation from the totalist psychology of the community has been of inestimable therapeutic value.

I have observed a common emotional experience that befalls many JWs as they attend their annual three-day conventions. Devout JWs conclude the weekend with fresh conviction to try again in earnest to meet WTS's rigorous standards wholly and completely. They show excited determination to correct their spiritual failings. Like a New Year's resolution, the untenable goal inevitably fails to materialize and the excitement of reaching the organization's high standards fizzles into disappointment when they realize that they have missed the mark once again. The JW is on an endless treadmill of Bible reading, meeting attendance, Christian association, prayer, and meditation – all in an effort to fight off their sinful nature and reach an elusive and illusory spiritual goal.

The effect upon the Western psyche of the Christian belief in inherited human sinfulness reaches its tentacles beyond religion to our very self-concept and the vocabulary we use to describe ourselves. Popular positive psychology encourages us to accept our flaws. But based upon what standard are we flawed? Against what ideological epitome of human existence are we measured? Any such measure is illusory. There exists no moral gauge that determines an individual's deservedness of life. In our evolving species, the only metrics of success towards which organisms reach are those dictated by our evolutionary predisposition to the success of our genome. Any remaining illusion of ideal human conduct or self-representation is residue from our ancient creeds of religious morality.

Psychologists work tirelessly with individuals whose feelings of self-loathing cause them significant mental illness in the form of depression and anxiety. Because of their inability to live up to an epitomic standard of existence, clients begin to feel that they do not deserve to experience joy. Feelings of worthlessness become a self-fulfilling prophecy as they subconsciously make decisions that sabotage their future happiness. I have experienced this state and do not wish it upon anyone.

As society's acceptance of secularism and the spiritual implications of evolutionary psychology spreads, we will see more people releasing their minds from bondage to destructive religious ideology. We experience life as one of billions of organisms dancing in a structureless, purposeless existence. We may be more intelligent than snakes and dogs—but our brains have unmistakable similarities. Humans are not made in God's image. We cannot know that we are any more or less spiritually inclined than snakes and dogs. Mythology and morality are figments of the collective human imagination. All of us face the absurdity of finding meaning in a meaningless existence. These philosophical concepts are hard to accept when our religious upbringing has lullabied us into a false sense of security. But when accepted, they wipe self-hatred off the psychological map and challenge the mind to expand beyond the fictitious limits of our ignorance.

The emphasis on unity and brotherhood in WTS may come at the expense of meaningful individual actualization. Humanist psychologist Abraham Maslow theorized that a person naturally aims to reach their individualized and fully actualized self (Maslow, 1943). Similarly, Bertrand Russell commented that the creative individuality of man is indeed our highest calling (Russell, 1917). Conversely, in WTS responsibility for the community's philosophical progress is abdicated to the Faithful & Discreet Slave and members are restricted in the extent to which they can pursue their individualized creative potential.

JWs are taught to reject worldly notoriety and the styles and trends embraced by larger society. Such rhetoric discourages the daring pursuits of JW creatives and carries the connotation that artistic and expressive inclinations are at odds with spiritual development. I have noticed that creatives among the community find these restrictions burdensome, either consciously or unconsciously. Elders warn that self-expression that incorporates modern artistic trends can "damage the consciences of the friends" ("the friends" is a colloquial insider expression used to refer to other JWs). If it is decided by elders that a member is causing a stir in the congregation for non-conforming styles of clothing, grooming, or artistic expression, he will be counseled for being a "cause for stumbling". If compliance is not demonstrated, he will be removed from positions of status in the congregation. When the natural inclination toward individual exploration and creative fulfillment is stifled, as is the case in ideologically totalist communities such as WTS, depression may result.

Of course, rather than weakening a collective mission, individualization promotes specialization of expertise that can be integrated toward intellectual depth and social stability in a community, leading to positive outcomes. As an artist and academic writer, I object to the proliferation of doctrine that is aimed at the stifling of the creative spirit. No doubt, many PIMOs feel the same.

When Regulation is Necessary

If there is one call to action in this book it is for policymakers to give attention to necessary regulation of organizations, be they religious or otherwise, that formalize the promulgation of doctrine and policy that are linked to negative psychological outcomes.

To be clear, no conclusive research categorically links JWs to mental health disorders. Some research has been performed to explore this hypothesis—research that has been cited extensively by the ex-JW community online. However, titillating as these studies may be for those whose lives and minds have been ravaged by WTS theology, they simply do not meet the robust standards of research required to pronounce causation.

Surely, not all extremes of thought must be regulated. It appears to be the natural state of the human mind to drift between extremes in a zigzag path toward a more moderate viewpoint that is conducive to psychological equilibrium at the individual level. Strict restriction of expression can impede this process. But when rhetoric containing cognitive distortions is formalized and belief in it is coerced, a person may find themselves trapped in an organization that systematically teaches them to believe things that are bad for their mental health.

Consider an illustration from biological medical science. When research irrefutably linked nicotine to negative health outcomes, cigarette companies were legislated and compelled to make consumers aware of the harmful potential of their product. People are still allowed to smoke, but not without adequate warning from the surgeon general. If research irrefutably links a religion's theology to cognitive distortions that have been proven to cause mental illness, and the group employs captive policies, should not prospective members be informed of the religion's potential to damage mental health? Is it time to put a surgeon general's warning on the front door of HDRGs?

I offer my ethical analysis to demonstrate the nature of the conflict that faces disillusioned JWs. When awakening from the psychological state created by regular involvement in an ideologically totalist community, PIMOs may for the first time become aware of the ethically questionable actions of their community. But they do not wish to be excommunicated from their family and friends, nor do they want to cause them unnecessary suffering by disassociating. Because of shunning policies, PIMOs are forced to decide between free expression of their ethical values and continued association with their loved ones.

It is time to take a closer look at the religious freedoms of PIMOs.

5. An Introduction to Religious Trauma Syndrome (RTS)

The *Diagnostic and Statistical Manual of Mental Disorders* (DSM) is a manual published by the American Psychiatric Association (APA) that guides mental health professionals as they assess and diagnose mental disorders. The most current version, the DSM-5, was published in 2013. An updated version, the DSM-6, is the result of a fourteen-year revision process of the DSM-5 and is scheduled to be completed in 2022.

The DSM-5 does not include Religious Trauma Syndrome (RTS).

Hey, APA. Put it in.

The term RTS was coined by psychotherapist Marlene Winell, Ph.D., author of *Leaving the Fold*, a self-help guide for spiritual recovery after leaving an oppressive religion. In a three-part series of articles published in the British journal *Cognitive Behaviour Therapy Today*, Winell provides anecdotal evidence gathered from her over twenty-five years of experience helping individuals facing post-traumatic stress resulting from breaking ties with their faith. On her website *journeyfree.org*, Winell provides a definition of RTS and an overview of the symptoms:

> Religious Trauma Syndrome is the condition experienced by people who are struggling with

leaving an authoritarian, dogmatic religion and coping with the damage of indoctrination. They may be going through the shattering of a personally meaningful faith and/or breaking away from a controlling community and lifestyle. The symptoms compare most easily with post-traumatic stress disorder (PTSD), which results from experiencing or being confronted with death or serious injury which causes feelings of terror, helplessness, or horror. This can be a single event or chronic abuse of some kind. With RTS, there is chronic abuse, especially of children, plus the major trauma of leaving the fold. Like PTSD, the impact of RTS is long-lasting, with intrusive thoughts, negative emotional states, impaired social functioning, and other problems. (Winell, 2006)

Faith deconstruction is not an uncommon reality of the human experience. For this reason, crises of faith may be dismissed as a natural part of personal development; a necessary albeit painful step. Many know the experience of holding firm religious affiliation only to be compelled by changing circumstances, growing knowledge, and perspective-broadening life experiences to reframe their belief systems. They go on to live healthy and socially integrated lives. However, the peculiarities of closed religious communities and NRMs increase the severity of this process such that it may lead to PTSD. As Winell puts it: "people who have not survived an authoritarian fundamentalist indoctrination do not realize what a complete mind-rape it really is" (Winell, 2006).

The severity of RTS is based on several factors. One is

the religiosity of the sufferer. A nominal member of any religion will experience significantly less psychological suffering from losing their faith than will devout members of the same religion. Another factor is the characteristics of the religion itself. RTS is much less likely to occur in the followers of religions with porous doctrinal boundaries and loose implementation of church policy. In these religions, individual members absorb new information at their own pace and create amalgamations of new learning and old doctrine to form a unique personal belief system that they find sustainable.

This chapter highlights some pertinent points from Winell's work as it relates to JWs. Additionally, I will heavily reference the article "The Shattered Spiritual Self: A Philosophical Exploration of Religious Trauma" by Murray State University assistant professor of philosophy Michelle Panchuk. Panchuk draws excellent connections between RTS, PTSD, and C-PTSD and provides a moral argument for an RTS survivor's "non-culpable failure to worship God" (Panchuk, 2018).

In the final section of this chapter, I seek to expand the discussion of RTS by including recent neurological research into moral injury PTSD. This subset of PTSD results from the trauma of transgressing personally held moral imperatives. Moral injury PTSD has relevance for individuals suffering from RTS, particularly those who were heavily involved in NRMs and HDRGs.

RTS, PTSD, and C-PTSD

Connecting RTS with PTSD contributes to a greater understanding of its severity. Thanks to the growing understanding of PTSD among veterans of foreign wars over the past few decades, the public is well aware of how destructive PTSD can be both for patients and their loved ones. In the next chapter, I will provide a narrative description of my personal experience with these symptoms. To start, it would be appropriate to delineate the symptoms clearly:

Intrusive thoughts, anxiety attacks, depression, preoccupation with suicide, sleep disorders, and substance abuse.

PTSD results from a traumatic experience, which the DSM-5 defines as "exposure to actual or threatened death, serious injury, or sexual violence" (APA, 2013). Such is the case with war veterans, who face literal near-death experiences, and victims of acts of sexual violence. PTSD can even be caused by a single traumatic event. This event is called the index trauma. A single index trauma may cause long-lasting and ongoing symptoms like the ones listed above, particularly if left untreated.

But what about *repeated* experiences of traumatic events? Panchuk says:

> Because many clinicians and psychologists believe that the current diagnosis criteria for PTSD fail to capture the unique harms of ongoing and repetitive trauma, (…) they have suggested

creating a unique category of traumatic experience commonly referred to as *complex trauma* (Panchuk, 2018, p.507)

Included in a list of experiences that might lead to complex trauma are:

> A history of subjection to totalitarian control over a prolonged period (months to years). Examples include hostages, prisoners of wars, concentration camp survivors, and survivors of some religious cults. (Herman, 2015, p.121)

So, whereas PTSD can be the result of one traumatic experience, C-PTSD includes the same symptoms but results from repeated and ongoing trauma. RTS is symptomatically the same as PTSD and C-PTSD but narrows the index trauma (or traumas) to religious affiliation and the loss of faith.

Panchuk also expands upon Winell's discussion in a way that is particularly relevant to the PIMO experience:

> Just as victims of domestic violence and child abuse can experience symptoms of post-traumatic distress while they are still trapped in the abusive relationship, so too a victim of religious trauma may experience symptoms of religiously significant post-traumatic distress while still identifying themselves with the religion in question. (Panchuk, 2018, p.516).

In sum, when a PIMO experiences the wholescale loss of

their belief system, symptoms of PTSD may result even while the individual still maintains active membership with the religious group.

As mentioned in the previous two chapters, it is my opinion that the WTS environment meets the qualifications of an ideologically totalist community. Additionally, disillusioned members may experience psychological distress resulting from the enforced repression of their sexual identity, violations of their religious freedoms, or fear of disfellowshipping and enforced shunning by their only social support system. This environment may lead to traumatic experiences for disillusioned members and result in symptoms of PTSD, including anxiety attacks, suicidal ideation, sleep disturbance, and risk of substance abuse. Further, the symptoms of RTS are not exclusive to those who choose to leave the organization. Disillusioned members who choose to remain, although they no longer agree with JW doctrine or WTS policy, namely PIMOs, suffer RTS in silence.

The Shattered Self and the Shattered Worldview

After decades of repeating my tired psychological defenses of JW doctrine in the face of new information and the evidence of science, academia, and my intuition, I came to the point where I simply knew too much to defend the belief system that I so cherished.

I remember when my worldview shattered. It was not a pleasant experience. It was only after several months of mindfulness practice that I learned to be comfortable with the pleasant openness of consciousness that occurs when one releases the defensive ego to the mysterious calm of universal entropy. But my initial awareness that everything I thought I knew about myself and the world could be completely wrong was terrifying. Such is the experience of the shattered self and shattered worldview that is sufficiently traumatic to cause months or years of PTSD symptoms.

This shattering of the self centers around what Winell calls the "paradoxical view of self."

> The religious version of "self is worthy" is usually a paradoxical view of the self which is both sinful and special. That is, an individual has nothing intrinsic to be proud of but can have great purpose, and can play a role in the cosmic spiritual drama. (Winell, 2006)

This is, of course, a recipe for narcissism. Narcissism is often a reactive arrogance to deep subconscious feelings of worthlessness and shame. The deep shame of JWs is their inherited Adamic sinfulness. JWs are taught that as a result of Adam's sin in the garden of Eden, all humans have imperfection in their very DNA, like a genetically inherited disease. Thus each JW is painfully aware of their private misdeeds and errant thoughts that provide daily evidence that they are worthy of everlasting death. As the Bible book of Romans states, "the wages sin pays is death" (Romans 6:23, Watch Tower 2013a). This private shame is only assuaged by obsessive reassurance of their special position in the eyes of Jehovah God, the Creator of the Universe as his chosen people; a reassurance that is doled out generously by the organization.

As discussed earlier, JWs believe that they represent the one true religion on earth. They also believe that association with WTS is the only acceptable way to worship God. Allow me to demonstrate the effect this may have on an individual's self-concept. Imagine that you are a baptized JW and I remind you that there are only 8.5 million JWs worldwide among the 7.8 billion people in the world. That means that you are close to the top 1 percentile in the world! You are 1 out of 100! Now, imagine that you have been granted by the organization (and thus by God's holy spirit) to a special title or responsibility, elevating you to spiritual leadership over your brethren. But then, just to be sure that you don't get a big head, you are incessantly reminded of your sinfulness in the eyes of God. This vicious cycle of spiritual elitism and private shame is not conducive to psychological balance or a healthy self-concept.

Often, when an outsider at work or school asks a JW to introduce themselves, the first thing they say in response, before mentioning family roles, hobbies, interests, or individual passions, is "I am one of Jehovah's Witnesses." Such is the prominence that belonging to WTS has in the self-concept of a devout JW. To be a JW, however, one must believe in God, the Bible, and WTS theology. If a member can no longer sustain such beliefs, he is no longer one of Jehovah's Witnesses. The disillusioned member is faced with the deafening question, who am I?

The disillusioned JW has lost their "role in a cosmic, spiritual drama" (Winell, 2006) Prior to awakening, the question of the meaning and purpose of life was no mystery. They preached the succinct answer to this question since they were tall enough, on tippy-toes, to reach a doorbell.

> Actually, the purpose of life can be expressed in just a few words: *We are here to learn about God and to do his will.* The Bible says: "The conclusion of the matter, everything having been heard, is: Fear the true God and keep his commandments. For this is the whole obligation of man."—Ecclesiastes 12:13. (Watch Tower, 1992, p. 8)

When neighbors in the door-to-door ministry refused to accept this trite philosophy, the JW returned to their car in bewilderment; puzzled as to how someone could be so ignorant and haughty that they would refuse to accept such a straightforward truth. The dramatic and wholescale loss of such a cherished purpose is utterly soul-crushing.

Along with the shattered self comes the shattered worldview. WTS doctrine touches on every aspect of life: family relationships, marriages, choices of career, social groups, and interactions with non-witnesses. Additionally, guidance on every major life decision is provided either by a quick search on *Watchtower Online Library* or through consultation with congregation elders. WTS teaches that the strength of one's relationship with God is demonstrated in decisions both great and small. The organization provides information on how to dress, what to do for work, how to have sex, and how to keep your house clean. Given the intrusion of the religion into every matter of life, the loss of it leaves a gaping hole, and the disillusioned religionist is drowned by a flood of unfiltered data bursting forth from the now mysterious and frightening world around them. (More on the reconstruction of basic values in Chapter 7).

Betrayal Trauma

In Lifton's *Losing Reality*, he alludes to a reactive psychological phenomenon that occurs in response to thought reform. He noticed the tendency of disillusioned intellectuals who finally had the opportunity to speak out against the communist regime to suffer a complete one-eighty in their polarized thinking. He writes:

> (…) in a reform-saturated environment, there is the potential for a sudden reversal of sentiment, for the release of bitter emotions directed both at thought reform and at the regime that perpetuates it. Behind such a reversal lies the latent resentment that thought reform builds up in varying degrees within virtually all who are exposed to it. This resentment originates in a basic human aversion to excessive personal control (…) (Lifton, 2019, p.18)

This is not a shock to the long-time JW. If one has been in the organization for several years, they have surely heard stories of members who ignominiously exited the group and subsequently attempted by letter, social media, or other means to enlighten others with their newfound assessment of the organization's evils. It is not uncommon for JWs, initially very zealous supporters of WTS, to outspokenly air their grievances over a laundry list of organizational and doctrinal idiosyncrasies and frustrations when they leave. Ideologically totalist environments, Lifton says, "promote an emotional contagion—of resentment as well as enthusiasm" (Lifton, 2019, p.19). This reactive psychology suggests that ideologically totalist organizations such as WTS essentially turn individual adherents into powder kegs— easily ignited on the one hand to radical zealotry and bitter outspoken criticism on the other.

Winell addresses this phenomenon in what she calls Betrayal Trauma Theory. She explains that "many ex-believers have anger about the abuse of growing up in a world of lies. They feel robbed of a normal childhood, honest information, and opportunity to develop and thrive. They have rage because they dedicated their lives and gave up everything to serve God. They are angry about losing their families and their friends. They feel enormously betrayed" (Winell, 2011).

JWs are encouraged to live a simple life, to reject higher education, and to "repudiate ungodliness and worldly desires" (Titus 2:12, Watch Tower 2013a) such as the quest for material success or notoriety in the secular community. Many JWs give up opportunities for university education and intellectually stimulating careers. Others give up potential opportunities for love and sexual intimacy with non-witnesses. Devout JW women often deny their instinctive need to have a child to pursue theocratic goals (or perhaps out of fear that her child might one day reject their JW identity and be disfellowshipped). All of these sacrifices are based on the assumption that the only meaningful pursuits in life are those associated with WTS.

When the illusion evaporates, they are faced with the full weight of what they have given up. Of course, long-term goals of any sort come with sacrifices, but one can usually balance anything given up with a deep conviction in the value of the pursuit. But when the doctrinal underpinnings of a disillusioned JW's sacrifices are no longer substantial, many feel that they have been robbed of opportunities to live a full and meaningful life.

I'll never forget how betrayed I felt when I learned of the deceit surrounding the dating of the Jewish exile from Babylon. This might seem like an insignificant doctrinal peculiarity to many readers. But not so for JWs. Let me explain.

WTS teaches that JWs alone have the correct understanding of Bible chronology and that WTS alone declares internationally the significance of the year 1914 as the beginning of the "last days" (although the teaching was not uncommon among adherents of American's mid-19th-century Adventist movement). While flawed at more than one juncture, the prophetic calculation of Biblical chronology pointing to 1914 C.E as the year of Christ's enthronement in the heavens is intellectually stimulating, a source of great pride for JWs, and deeply impactful upon the life decisions of devout members. JWs base all of their biggest life decisions upon the belief that the last days began in 1914 and that the end of the world is coming soon; in their very lifetime.

Proceeding logically from this chronological foundation, JW teenagers reject scholarships, adult JWs reject employment opportunities and JW mothers forgo childbirth. All such sacrifices are based upon the understanding that the end is coming soon, and time is best spent saving as many outsiders as possible before the great war of Armageddon that will rid the earth of non-believers.

The whole chronology hinges on a pivotal date; a date mentioned in both biblical and secular history and therefore reconcilable with modern calendars. This pivotal date is the date of the Jewish exile from Babylon. WTS adamantly defends the date 607 BCE for this historical occurrence, despite the evidence presented by archeologists and historians for the date 587 BCE. In 1977, a JW named Carl Olof Jonsson published a scholarly work called *The Gentile Times Reconsidered* that addressed this debate with an exhaustive discussion of the archeological and historical evidence. Despite the implications for his personal faith, Jonsson courageously presented his scholarly research to the organization. As discussed in the memoir of the defrocked Governing Body member Raymond Franz, *Crisis of Conscience (1983)*, the board of leaders rejected the research. Jonsson was later disfellowshipped for apostasy. The corroborating accounts from both Jonsson and Franz strongly suggest that the Governing Body examined the new information, deliberately refused to release it to the rank and file, and summarily silenced Jonsson (Franz, 1983, p.199).

I trusted the Church's leadership with my entire life. But I had been persuaded to distrust and limit my exposure to legitimate academic research that would have profoundly affected my most important life decisions.

I was heartbroken. In that moment, I promised myself that I would never trust another human being again.

Moral Injury

With the following discussion, I seek to expand the definition of RTS to include what psychologists and neuroscientists are calling moral injury PTSD. Moral injury is a subset of PTSD that can occur along with RTS in members of High Control Groups, depending on the level of involvement in the religious group's ethically questionable policy. If indeed RTS is a Ballung concept as Panchuk suggests (a spectrum of conditions with family resemblances rather than a single disorder) (Panchuk, 2018, p.517), I would like to propose adding Moral Injury PTSD to the RTS family based on the discussion below of recent neurological findings and my personal experience with RTS.

The study of moral injury was born of PTSD research in combat veterans and was formally delineated in 2009 by Brett T. Litz et al. in an article highlighting the experience of soldiers who encountered "potentially morally injurious events, such as perpetrating, failing to prevent, or bearing witness to acts that transgress deeply held moral beliefs and expectations." According to the authors, these encounters were "deleterious in the long-term, emotionally, psychologically, behaviorally, spiritually, and socially" (Litz et al., 2009, p.695). Interestingly, in the clinical treatment of patients with PTSD, psychiatrists noted important differences in the narrative content of the soldiers' traumatic experiences. When veterans of twentieth-century wars are diagnosed with PTSD, it is most often because of lingering terror from a life-threatening experience. However, a minority of veterans with similar PTSD symptoms did not report such frightful content. Their trauma was based not on fear of violent death but on a violation of their moral code.

A striking example of this was noticed among operators of remotely piloted aircraft (RPA or drones) who, while facing no threat to their safety, experienced symptoms similar to those of combat PTSD. Research of these pilots showed that "the number of events in which RPA warfighters witnessed civilian bystanders being killed by enemy forces or felt shared responsibility for the injury or death of bystanders" were "significant predictors" of PTSD (Chapelle et al., 2019, p.86). RPA pilots were completely safe in military bunkers on United States soil, but they still struggled with the moral and ethical implications of their violent contribution to war. They were suffering symptoms of moral injury.

The idea that PTSD can be subdivided based on the nature of the trauma has inspired further study into the neurological footprints of various types of emotional content. Researchers refer to the trauma-inducing event or events as the "index trauma" (Barnes et al., 2019, p.98). Individuals can be categorized and studied based on specific characteristics of the index trauma. This allows for more focused research. In 2016, Boccia et al. "explored the possibility that different traumatic events produce different alterations in the PTSD neural network" (Boccia et al., 2016, p.226). Using positron emission tomography (PET) scans and functional magnetic resonance imaging (fMRI), they showed that not all PTSD is the same. Although they did not study moral injury directly, fMRI studies showed that when the index trauma is separated into the categories of combat, sexual abuse, and natural disaster, each activates different neural substrates. In short, different types of trauma cause different biological responses in the brain.

A fascinating study in 2019 using fMRI technology showed a difference in the resting-state brain fluctuation and functional connectivity of individuals with PTSD and those with moral injury (Sun et al., 2019). In this study, researchers ranked the intensity of the index trauma using the Clinician-Administered PTSD Scale (CAPS) for PTSD and the Moral Injury Events Scale (MIES) for moral injury. Then they measured spontaneous amplitude of low-frequency fluctuations (ALFF) and functional connectivity while the subject was in a state of rest. They concluded that "neural correlates of morally injurious events and symptoms as measured specifically by MIES and its subscales may be differentiated from the neural correlates of PTSD as measured by the CAPS" (Sun et al., 2019, p.448).

In other words, the biology of moral injury in the brain is distinctly different from that of PTSD. One significant finding in the above study relates to the function of the left inferior parietal lobule (L-IPL). The researchers concluded that "morally injurious events are correlated with resting-state brain responses in the L-IPL" but that they did not find this relationship in the scans of patients with fear-based index traumas. It appears that the L-IPL is the home of moral injury trauma. Interestingly, other differentiating characteristics were found in neurological activity dependent on whether the trauma was related to a moral transgression performed by the self or a moral transgression performed by someone else.

Neurological research into moral injury using brain-scanning technologies such as fMRI is in its infancy and much is yet to be understood. But the progress in this field has profound implications. With its focus on the emotion of fear, PTSD can be a reductive diagnosis that does not directly address the moral component of traumatic events. The multifaceted emotional experience of combat veterans speaks to this inadequacy. Upon returning home, veterans are often praised for service to their country. They may be left alone to carry not only fearful memories of battle but also the traumatic moral burden of the violent acts they performed in support of an ideology. To reduce their psychological symptoms to combat PTSD can render the moral injury untreated.

Something similar may happen to disillusioned JWs, who must reckon with the implications of their actions during the time they spent with the group and their involvement in the dissemination and implementation of ethically questionable doctrines and policies. To some extent, this may occur in all awakening JWs. To varying degrees, every member has contributed to the social environment of the community; they have shunned disfellowshipped members, lent their voice to the organization's biased rhetoric about outsiders, and proliferated misinformation. However, moral injury is most likely to occur among two subsets of members: 1) those who have played a significant role in the conversion of new members (called

Regular Pioneers), and 2) those who have administered coercive policy (congregation elders).

WTS has varying echelons of service, generally based on the number of hours that one contributes to the proselytizing work. Some of these designations are auxiliary pioneer (30–50 hours/month), regular pioneer (70 hours/month), and special pioneer or missionary, who receive a small stipend for living expenses (130 hours/month). Much of the effort of these highly active JWs is centered on the door-to-door evangelizing work with an emphasis on starting Bible Studies. A Bible Study is the one-on-one tutoring of an interested neighbor in WTS doctrine. As stated in the book *Fully Accomplish Your Ministry*, used as the basis for week-long training sessions for regular pioneers (colloquially called the "Pioneer Book"), "our primary objective is to help people become baptized disciples of Christ Jesus" (Watch Tower, 2014b).

Pioneers devote many hours to their work of bringing a Bible student "into the truth." Discussions usually begin with a series of weekly doorstep visits to discuss a scriptural question with the householder. Then, doorstep Bible discussions are transitioned into the home. Instructions on how to do this are given in the *Watchtower*:

> Start by lengthening those doorstep studies (…) When the householder feels comfortable with a longer visit, ask him if there is some place where you can sit down together and continue the discussion (…) Eventually, to accelerate his progress, you might even ask the student if he would be willing to study twice a week (Watch Tower, 2020b)

The pioneer will continue to develop the relationship, gradually introducing prayer at the beginning and end of study sessions. An effort is also made to show evidence that WTS is the religious organization chosen by God in modern times. It is the pride of many pioneers when one of their spiritual disciples decides to dedicate their lives to Jehovah and become a baptized JW.

But if a Regular Pioneer becomes disillusioned with their faith and religious organization, moral injury may result when they begin to comprehend the weight of their undue influence on the Bible student. Missionaries and special pioneers may have led dozens to baptism over decades of faithful service. It is no wonder that many who leave the organization feel the need to correct any misinformation and uninformed advice they gave their protégés in their religious fervor.

Worse still is the experience of the JW elder, who may have been involved in administering WTS policies that directly impact the health and safety of lay-witness. For example, congregation elders are responsible for implementing the judicial and disfellowshipping process at the local level. Imagine what it feels like to awaken to the realization that in your ignorance, you enforced a ruling that permanently separated mother from daughter, son from father, or brother from sister.

As a PIMO who has served as an elder, I too must reckon with this guilt. Moral injury compounded the effects of my RTS. All at once, I experienced artificially induced internal guilt for disloyalty to God, genuine human guilt for breaking apart families through disfellowshipping, shame for being a JW, and shame for being a deceitful PIMO. It was overwhelming.

Some elders serve on Hospital Liaison Committees (HLC) sponsored by WTS. As was discussed in Chapter 4, the HLC is meant to support JWs in their decision to abstain from blood when undergoing serious medical treatment. However, as previously noted, HLCs could be interpreted as an extension of the organization's undue influence on a patient at the very hospital bed. If an awakening JW elder begins to disbelieve the organization's doctrine on the sanctity of blood, they might experience intense symptoms of moral injury at the responsibility they bear for persuading others to reject organizationally unsanctioned forms of medical treatment. This, of course, would especially be the case if an elder had unduly influenced a decision to refuse blood-based treatment that resulted in the loss of life.

When the Jehovah's-Witnesses-are-the-manifestation-of-God's-organization-on-earth Jenga piece is removed from the stack, the whole tower of belief comes crashing down. Along with the destruction comes crushing guilt over one's personal contribution to human suffering.

6. A PIMO Faces Religious Trauma Syndrome

It was a mundane disturbance that awoke me from sleep, perhaps a cell phone vibration notifying me of a new text message. But as my mind transitioned from sleep to conscious awareness, the gravity of my circumstances and the complexities of my lifestyle of dedication to an organization that I could no longer support crashed upon me with tsunami strength. There were no particularly new appearances in consciousness in that moment that I had not already wrestled with over the past six months. But on this particular night, they seemed to converge with newfound ferocity. And in my groggy half-slumber, my tired psychological resources were caught off guard, unprepared to level a theological defense.

I sat in the tiny living room of my one-bedroom apartment and observed as the sensations of my sympathetic nervous system took over. Tingling and numbness overcame my left arm and hand. "Classic symptoms of heart attack," I thought. Then came the racing heartbeat. I checked my pulse. It was well above the number on the heart-rate monitor attached to the elliptical machine at the gym that alerts the user to slow down.

I woke my wife up from sleep. "Call 9-1-1."

She did.

"Babe. I love you. I've always loved you," I said.

The uncontrollable shivering, more violent than the kind produced by winter's cold, arrived at the same time as the ambulance. Terror crept through my every vein and produced a cold sweat at my temples. The ambulance left. The shaking didn't for a few more hours.

There is something special about your first; your first panic attack. It turns out that you are not dying, even though you feel like you are and wish that you were. But the sudden awareness of your inability to control your body's physiological reaction to panic is a stark realization of your psychological fragility. The experience is life-changing.

The EMT told me to get some Xanax from my general practitioner, who happily obliged, ignoring my reticent comments about a crisis of faith.

"Is it okay to be using this stuff every day?" I asked the good doctor.

"Yeah, you'll be fine," he answered. "You seem like a responsible guy."

Thanks, mainstream American medical system. Sounds like a great solution to long-term symptoms of existential crisis. At least now I have clout with the hip-hop community.

My first panic attack was neither the beginning nor the end of my journey through RTS. But it was a wake-up call. It is hard to deny that something is wrong when you are at the peak of physical health but find yourself calling Emergency Services in the middle of the night. Still, I continued to ignore my psychological symptoms for months hoping to protect my beloved faith. Eventually, you learn to sense an oncoming panic attack before it manifests in the full-blown symptoms described above. You learn to catch it early, take a Xanny, and if you get the timing just right, the drug will hit at just the moment that the anxiety crescendos.

Let's rewind a bit.

Necessary Vagaries and Deepening Involvement

Testimonials of ex-witnesses abound on the internet. Exhaustive video autobiographies proliferate on YouTube. The fact that ex-JWs are compelled to provide such intimate narratives of leaving the organization is evidence that the subjective experience strikes an individual to the very core. For victims, chronicling their journey through adverse religious experience (ARE) is cathartic and contributes to their recovery from the pain of ending their association with WTS.

To the outsider who has not experienced these troubles, and perhaps even to the ex-member who has grown to integrate into a larger community, such belabored stories can appear self-indulgent. However, it is important to remember that JWs see themselves as characters in a "cosmic spiritual drama" (Winell, 2011). Thus, the grieving ex-member initially interprets their personal experiences as one of universal gravity and importance. This dramatic worldview is indicative of the underdeveloped psyches of individuals who leave such groups and takes some time to wear off.

I admit to such fantastical thinking in the early days of my awakening. However, in an attempt to relate to a broader audience, I have limited the discussion of details of my organizational responsibilities that would only be meaningful to ex-JWs and PIMOs. Indeed, moderating one's understanding of the significance of personal trauma is a crucial step in overcoming it: honoring your pain, giving it the spotlight for a time, and then allowing it to find its humble place in the great symphony of human suffering performed over the millennia of our species' existence.

Additionally, my spiritual views have changed considerably along my journey. In the initial days of my religious deconstruction, I clutched desperately at belief in the existence of my best friend, my Heavenly Father and Creator of the Universe, Jehovah. Although such reluctance to reckon with the possibility of divine nonexistence is no longer a hindrance to my spiritual journey, you will notice this reluctance in my journal entries. Further, as I explained at length in the introduction, I am being vague intentionally and omitting certain identifying details of my memoir to protect my anonymity. I have also changed and redacted names to protect the innocent.

My ideological commitment and psychological entwining with WTS proceeded in stages of increasing depth over the years. It is not uncommon for the persuasion of an individual and their integration within a closed community to occur in phases, critical moments of submission, and recommitment. Most readers will be familiar with the concept of "losing oneself" in a relationship, social group, or perhaps even a career. The case of the devout JW who loses his or her individuality gradually, over time, and with incremental loss of personal identity could indeed be interpreted this very same way.

Pivotal moments of internal conflict and subsequent compliance with WTS norms are also relevant to my experience: the rejection of higher education, the choice to become a full-time evangelizer, the acceptance of positions of oversight, and even formal contractual relationships with legal entities used by WTS. All such commitments served to deepen my conviction and intensify the traumatic and life-changing impact of RTS upon disillusionment.

As discussed in Chapter 2, at baptism one gives oneself over to the organization. "Being totally immersed in water is a fitting symbol of their dying to their former self-seeking course of life" (Watch Tower, 1998, p. 6). But despite completely giving yourself to the organization, one is not privy to all of the details of involvement at baptism. Further information regarding organizational policy and structure is stratified based on the hierarchical role of individual members. The lay-witness has a largely different idea of the deliberations of local elder's bodies than does the elder himself (and perhaps the wife and children of an elder who see firsthand the conflict their husbands and fathers experience as a result of their congregational responsibilities). It could be postulated that rank-and-file JWs might even be less informed than some outsiders, given their loyalty to the Governing Body's prohibition on visiting websites of former members. The inquisitive non-JW researcher (or PIMO) can access procedural and oversight documents on the internet (such as *Shepherd the Flock of God*, letters to congregation elders, and WTS Branch Office procedural documents) with a simple Google search. This information is under lock and key for the average JW. An advancing JW is kept in the dark about this kind of information until they are considered to be of mature enough spirituality to see such sensitive material. It is not a matter of spirituality, of course, but a matter of loyalty to the organization that must be proven over time.

Becoming a congregation elder can be a jarring experience for a young man; perhaps as young as twenty-five. The announcement of appointment in the congregation is usually marked by congratulations and even celebration by close family and friends. It is a significant milestone in a JW man's life. But it also represents a certain reckoning with the indelicacies of the organization's judicial process and the possible lack of unity in the elder body. The political atmosphere, while common among groups of men in leadership roles, can be shocking and somewhat disillusioning to a new elder. The childlike and spiritually minded young man is thrust into deliberations about appropriate disciplinary responses to various behavioral infractions of congregation members.

In a short time, the new elder is trained to sit on judicial committees along with more experienced elders. This can be a grueling experience, traumatic not only for the victim of the humiliating procedure but also for the new elder, who faces social pressure from his spiritual mentors and father figures to dole out the punishment.

> "I'm sorry, but I need to ask you a few more questions, Brother," the new elder asks an older man under interrogation who, just months before, was his respected spiritual advisor. "What exactly was the content of the pornography that you viewed? Did it include homosexuality or bestiality? Was it accompanied by the unclean practice of masturbation? Have you informed your wife?"

I shudder now to think of it.

Or on another occasion, while addressing a disgraced teenager who sits before a committee of three elders in the infamous "back room" of the Kingdom Hall:

> "Thank you for waiting outside while we deliberated on your situation. Forgive me for bringing this up again. But we have to be completely sure that what happened is included under the Society's definition of the Greek word *porneia.* Did you simply *touch* her vagina once? Or did you massage or manipulate it with the intention of arousing her sexually?"

Then,

> "Thanks for clarifying. Could you go wait outside again while the committee discusses this a bit more? We will let you know in a few minutes what our decision is."

The outcome, of course, is either shaming by way of reproof or disfellowshipping.

I was that young elder. Memories such as these lie at the root of my moral injury.

The cognitive dissonance of stepping into the role of disciplinarian over your peers and friends requires work to reconcile. As the theory of cognitive dissonance suggests, one must address the conflict by adjusting existing beliefs or adding new ones. Lifton's thought-terminating clichés have their moment as more experienced men comfort the new elder with fabrications about "seeing the direction of Jehovah's holy spirit" during the judicial proceedings. Or worse still, elders may placate their conflicted consciences by reminding themselves that they were simply "following the direction of mother," as some loyal JWs refer to the organization's leadership. Thanks to ongoing mentorship from older elders, the new elder's doubts and concerns gradually fade. Consequently, the man's devotion to the organization and psychological attachment to his comrade elders strengthen.

The developing JW takes deep pride in and receives great praise for his organizational accomplishments. Administrative or educational assignments are interpreted as evidence of Jehovah's blessing and the answer to private prayers for favor. Indeed, personal pride in theocratic achievements and interpretation of them as evidence of God's approval makes relinquishing them so much more traumatic. Truth be told, after initially winning such battles over my discursive empathy for outsiders and less devout brethren, my experience of finding favor within my religious community was grand. Some of the most precious memories of my formative years center around the privileges of service I received in support of the WTS mission. It is only after much post-RTS therapy and self-reflection that I can reapproach memories of my organizational accomplishments in WTS, see past my grief, and take some personal pride in them.

The many beautiful memories of service to my God, Jehovah, shoulder-to-shoulder with my spiritual brothers make the trauma of waking up so much harder to transcend.

Researching Doubts

Doubts are not uncommon to people of faith. Given the rigidity of the belief system in the face of ever-changing social norms, it is safe to say that each JW has faced their fair share of religious uncertainty. WTS encourages JWs to "make the truth their own" (Watch Tower, 2014c) and to reason logically about their beliefs. This is a surprisingly bold prescription given that the very process of examining and reexamining one's beliefs can lead to a complete deconstruction of the faith; possibly evidence that leadership is completely oblivious to the logical fallacies of WTS theology. Whatever the case, the solution to feelings of doubt is addressed in the *Watchtower*: "How, then, can we protect ourselves from damaging doubts? The answer is remarkably simple: by firmly rejecting satanic propaganda and fully availing ourselves of God's provisions to make us 'solid in the faith'" (Watch Tower, 2001).

Remarkably, WTS does not advocate ignoring doubts, but rather rigorous intellectual battle. Notice further advice given in the face of doubt:

> Fight doubts vigorously (...) "Are we living in the last days? Can you believe everything the Bible says? Is this truly Jehovah's organization?" Satan would love to plant doubts like these in your mind. Do not let a negligent attitude towards spiritual feeding leave you easy prey to his deceptive teachings. (Colossians 2:4–7) Follow the advice given to Timothy. Be a good student of "the holy writings" so that you can "continue in the things that you learned and were persuaded to believe" (Watch Tower, 2001).

Yes, WTS encourages JWs to keep proving their faith to themselves. However, given that all information published by outsiders is potentially "satanic propaganda," the doubter is left to trust only the research tools provided by the organization. A JW's lack of trust in outside material is compounded by a complete lack of confidence in their own ability to stand up to opposing influence from outsiders. Thus, the awakening JW is in a special kind of intellectual darkness. They no longer unequivocally believe the writings of WTS. But they deeply distrust literature produced by non-witnesses. I faced the challenge of navigating decades' worth of literature from WTS archives; digging through the repetitious rhetoric searching for nuggets of new truth that could help resolve my psychological dissonance.

In my case, this intellectual figure-of-eight only contributed to worsening symptoms. The arguments were tired. There was no publication left that I had not annotated, dissected, and prayerfully meditated upon. Although I was afraid to read secular literature, I could usually get a sense of outside theological, philosophical, and scientific arguments from the introductory paragraphs of WTS articles written in response to popular criticisms. Later, as my critical reading skills improved, I began to see the logical fallacies. Even in the dearth of outside voices, the pseudo-intellectual arguments of WTS regarding creationism, the age of *Homo sapiens*, microevolution, the great flood, and the dating of the Bible began to fall apart.

The Onset of PTSD Symptoms

The onset of PTSD symptoms began on a special weekend of organizational training. I was in a Kingdom Hall full of my fellow elders, watching an instructional video as it played on the big-screen TV at the front of the room. The video showed a group of three elders discussing whether or not a JW woman should be allowed to continue in her role as a regular pioneer. (Being removed as a pioneer can be considerably distressing to someone who has centered their life around the privilege.) Once a year, elders meet to decide if pioneers who did not meet the 840-hour yearly time commitment will be allowed to continue. The video reenactment was a sample discussion of an exemplary body of elders who were meeting to discuss such a decision. Below is my journal entry on the subject:

> If this is all fake, then this video is ridiculous! What does it matter?! Not only is pioneering not mentioned in the scriptures, but surely the

hours upon hours of elders' meetings required to make judgments about who can pioneer is even further removed from true spirituality. And then think about the time and money (from volunteer contributions) that it took to prepare a professional video to teach the elders how to act when they are making decisions!

Of all the things that one could fault the religion for, this is not a significant one. But it was enough to evaporate what was left of my belief that my religious organization was backed by the Almighty Sovereign of the Universe.

That day, on the drive home with a fellow elder, terrified by the thought of losing my faith, my family, and my community all at once, the initial symptoms of RTS struck. It is hard to describe what it was like, as a peace-loving, pacifist Bible-thumper who had never even permitted himself to watch a Rated-R movie, to experience the onset of homicidal ideation. Without Jehovah to protect me from my sinful nature, could I be a murderer? Mental images of slashing my best friend's neck with a meat cleaver came on strong; repeating over and over and over again. I had nobody to pray to, no record of personally defined and implemented morality to draw from, nobody to confide in.

It is not a big jump from homicidal ideation to suicidal ideation. If I was a danger to my loved ones, better I take myself out before anyone else got hurt. If you have never had the experience in consciousness of suicidal imagery, it is truly alarming at first. Flashes in consciousness of my wrists slit with a broken record and bleeding over the edge of a bathtub (likely a subconscious replaying of my first introduction to the concept of suicide in a film I saw as a child) punished me on an hourly basis. As in the case of all compulsive thoughts, the thinker then enters a vicious cycle. First, the suicidal image enters consciousness followed by the affective sensation of fear which then triggers a heightened stress response. As a result of the stress response, the intrusive suicidal thoughts appear to gain strength—starting the cycle all over again. It is hard to sleep. A bit like sharing the bed with your own murderer. Sleeping pills help. You wake up in the morning and immediately think, "Hey, maybe today I won't have those thoughts." But then they come back. Just a flash at first. And the cycle begins again. I could muscle the thoughts to the back of my mind with mundane morning duties until about noon. But the images would inevitably come back.

Sometimes, the intrusive thoughts I experienced centered around my fear of becoming an apostate and turning on the organization, being disloyal to Jehovah and my brothers, and maybe even writing a book about it. "I'm not an apostate, I'm not an apostate, I'm not an apostate," I would scream, pounding my steering wheel repeatedly during a lunch break from work. Every day, I made a new commitment to Jehovah; a re-dedication. But by noon, the rebellious thoughts would appear again. Half a Xanax to make them go away long enough to give a public talk at the Kingdom Hall. Then another half to get to sleep. Rinse and repeat.

Getting Help

As elaborated before, I found myself in a situation where I was afraid both of those on the outside and those on the inside. The aforementioned psychological symptoms would be evidence enough for most that a trip to the doctor is in order. But given my commitment to the preaching work and determination to live a life of material simplicity, my financial situation was deplorable. Lack of funds was another roadblock to receiving professional mental health support.

Xanax enabled me to continue my theocratic duties: talks from the stage at the local Kingdom Hall, presentations before hundreds at larger JW conventions, and the full-time ministry. Daring to admit my blasphemous thoughts to family, friends, congregation elders and mentors of stature in the organization yielded no new spiritual insights that could ease my suffering. Worse yet, revealing my doubts put me in a very precarious position. I was unknowingly opening myself to the suspicions of my fellow JWs. Doing so aroused further scrutiny of my commitment to the group's mission.

For the first time, I began to realize why so many JWs had resisted my efforts to meet with them as part of my shepherding work as an elder. These in-home visits by two business-suited elders send a clear message: no matter who you are in the organization, you are not above the systematic efforts of leadership to insert themselves into your personal life and to attempt to convince you to comply.

I came to see the attention of congregation elders as a threat, not only to myself but also to my marriage. The overzealous men were approaching my wife at the congregation meetings when I was not present. I knew that they would quickly attempt to become emotional confidants for her and would interpret their intrusion into our private affairs as part of their spiritual responsibility; a reflection of Jehovah's concern for my wife in the dangerous spiritual environment that I was creating at home. As an elder, I had seen loyalties shift quickly in the past, even in the closest of marriages.

3/26/19

When the anxiety comes on strong, I know why. I'm afraid of something. Sometimes it's hard to figure out what I'm afraid of. But when I identify it, I can then approach it and think about a solution.

I think that is what I am afraid of right now:

That another man would "Shepherd" my wife and drive a religious wedge between us and that the elders at the Kingdom Hall will start turning on me.

So what's the work-around?

I've already made it clear that I do not need the elders to shepherd me and my wife. "I'll take it from here" was enough to reassert my role with my wife and the elders.

Eventually, I sought out therapy from outsider practitioners. At first, this only increased my symptoms. Every visit triggered a panic attack. Each visit brought further proof that my faith was crumbling. And worse yet, non-JW therapists tiptoed around matters of faith. In their liberal respect for religious freedom, they were reluctant to suggest that it was my religion itself that was causing me distress. This speaks to a greater problem for RTS sufferers in the therapy room: the unpreparedness of therapists to challenge a patients' destructive beliefs. Much academic literature centers around the *benefits* of faith to the recovery of trauma patients. But religion is, indeed, the opiate of the masses. And like all drugs of stupefaction, it is a short-term solution at best. Religion wasn't my way out. It was the cause of my suffering.

My mind bounced punishingly between what I saw as my only two options: leave the organization or kill myself. The former would cause immense long-term grief to my wife, my mother, my extended family, and anyone else whose happiness was tied up with my existence. The latter option would be interpreted by my loved ones as a symptom of mental illness, an illness that Jehovah would understand and forgive. My loved ones could maintain their faith in Jehovah's mercy and in seeing me again in a paradise in the future.

There was no middle road.

Unbeknownst to me, I was attempting to base my decision-making on what philosophers call utilitarianism. Utilitarianism, I came to find out much later, theorizes that the best decision is the one that yields the most happiness for the most people or reduces the most suffering for the most people. Death would yield less heartache for my loved ones than apostatizing. Suicide seemed like the best option.

It has been said that suicidality is the ultimate lack of imagination. I knew I could not go on as a JW. But, I could not imagine any alternatives to my existing lifestyle. I had thought everything through. I had an answer for everything. There was nothing left to learn.

Except that there was.

And there is a middle road. There are so many middle roads.

Finding the Middle Road

Finally, I connected with an RTS-informed therapist with considerable experience treating Jehovah's Witnesses. The introduction occurred with the kind of serendipity that would cause even the most stubbornly atheistic RTS survivor to retract all comments about the stupidity of religion and kneel in praise to the Almighty. Suffice to say, I finally felt heard.

It takes a special sort of courage to throw off the bonds of political correctness and therapeutic convention and level with a man; to fearlessly tell him what he is afraid to know; to tell him that faith is not always beneficial and that it is understandable that he would find his religion ethically troublesome. That he could still be good without God.

My therapist assured me that my situation was not new. I was not alone. She had seen this before. She got me to open up.

"You like music, right? Tell me about the Kingdom Melodies (JW hymns sung at weekly congregation meetings)," she said. "What do you think about the lyrics and melodies?"

"They are pretty lame," I replied.

This was her window of opportunity. She told me that other JWs also find it hard to speak negatively about WTS. She told me that holding well-founded criticisms does not mean that a person is disloyal. It is okay to be negative, she explained. In hindsight, this line of argument appears simplistic, but at the time, it was profoundly refreshing. My therapist then told her story of being raised in an NRM. She challenged me to see if I could maintain my criticality and individuality of thought and find a place of genuineness in the organization.

Genuineness. I had heard the word, but never given thought to my genuineness; integrity to myself.

I wanted life. I wanted to reduce suffering in the world, not to contribute to it. I had to find a middle road. I had to become PIMO.

> 12/1/18
>
> That seems like a good goal to me. The problem is that what is genuine to me is a whole lot less than

what I am doing [theocratically] now. Navigating my way down from my involvement in the organization is not going to be an easy task.

I think the best time to step down as an elder will be when we [my wife and I] relocate. Usually, an elder is deleted and reappointed. I can simply turn in my book as I leave. I will be deleted in one congregation and then not reappointed in the new one. I will not be asked to give advice based on a theology that I can no longer support. I will not be involved in coercion. I will not be involved in forced confession, public shaming, or excommunicating people from their family and friends. But I will still be able to keep an eye on the organization, keep my wife's respect, and make genuine friends that I can connect to on a level deeper than just doctrine.

But it's a long road. I don't know how soon we can move. There is the possibility that the brothers turn on me before I have the opportunity to leave.

My fears are based on some deep, deep but unhealthy conviction that I am a bad dude. Bound for evil if I am not restrained by my involvement with the organization. Undoing this belief in myself is hard.

I do not want my readers to misunderstand my message in *A Voice from Inside*. I am concerned that current and former members of NRMs will conclude that I am advocating that individuals remain within captive organizations, or worse, judging them for their decision to leave. This is not my intention. My decision was personal. Below, I have outlined my reasons for maintaining membership as a JW for the purpose of increasing awareness of the PIMO condition, and to provide interested readers with insight into what might cause this sociological phenomenon.

Suffice to say, there was a moment at the apex of my crisis, curled up in a fetal position on my bathroom floor and screaming through my tears at God, that I alighted upon a conviction welled up from the depths of my spiritual being. While everything else was a mystery, I was certain of one thing. I knew that I would not let any group of men permanently sever me from my family. That would be an act of presumptuousness on the part of WTS that I simply could not allow.

Furthermore, I must emphasize that my decision is temporary. My days of dedicating myself to a social movement or organization of any kind are behind me. The fact that I would be forced to make a permanent decision about my attendance at a place of worship is at the center of accusations that WTS is a captive organization. It is this very dichotomy that exacerbates RTS among PIMOs. As is universally the case, one must never abdicate responsibility for ethical matters to authoritarian figures. Balancing the processes of individualization and integration with society in a way that yields personal and community benefit is the challenge of a lifetime. I cannot say that the circumstances that allow me to remain as a JW today, will be the same tomorrow. I am PIMO for now.

Frankly, my reasons for remaining are not always clear even to myself. I wonder at what point I will face a challenge to my ethical integrity that forces me to break my silence before my peers and family. In the meantime, my search for the middle road has led me on a winding path of spiritual and psychological transcendence that has yielded superpowers that I never thought I could possess. More on this in Chapter 8.

1/29/19

Still, fears abound. Fear that I am an Apostate. That I am doing something wrong by staying in the organization. Or that I might use my knowledge to harm someone; to damage their faith.

Or worse yet, that I will lose myself again to the brainwashing.

I heard it in a movie once: the challenge is not finding truth, it's knowing what to do with it once you have it. It separates the men from the boys. At what point did the leaders of this organization learn what I have learned? Incrementally like a frog in boiling water? Coercive persuasion? Or was it like me? Left with the crippling weight of deciding the moral thing to do all by themselves.

Men from boys.

Just you and God, now. What will you do?

Tolerate. Not proliferate.

Last week I conducted a lesson from the

platform about "Jehovah's Organization," carefully wordsmithing my delivery so that I could sleep that night.

Frog in water.

How many men before me? After all, this is our wives and families at risk here. It would be so easy to turn a blind eye. Blame it on someone else, on the Faithful and Discreet Slave.

To become a self-liar. Then a real liar.

7. A Day in the Life of a PIMO

11/23/18

I'm just so mad that a cult-like organization could have such an iron grip on my life! It's so frustrating!!

I just want to relax and enjoy my life helping others and doing good for them. But I have this incessant dark cloud over my head. The worst part is that the fundamental teachings of the religion violate some of my most basic values. It can be exhausting to keep my head about this without getting soft. Cooling without softening.

It still feels like something is coming between my wife and me. If I ever get exhausted and have to step down as an elder, it will be hell all over again. I know how much it will hurt her.

The only thing that brings some relief is thinking about the people that I love. Right now I am surrounded by people that I can love and help. And I *do* love them: my wife, my family, her family, the congregation. If I were to lose patience, I would lose out on so many opportunities to show love.

Last night I was able to talk to Samuel [an acquaintance] at the Kingdom Hall. His wife, Emily, wants to kill herself. So does Sam's brother. Why?

Probably because they don't want to be in "The Truth." I get it. Me either. But without me on the inside, who would encourage them to get mental health treatment? What other JW will support help them as they face the fear that maybe (just maybe) they don't have everything they need within the organization? Who else can do that?!!!

It dawns on me that my position is an incredibly unique one. I cannot waste it just because I get lonely at night.

Living the High Demand Life

They don't call 'em High Demand Religious Groups for nothing. "Narrow is the way that leadeth unto life." Even for those for whom the indoctrination of the organization is most closely connected to their self-concept, it is a rigorous schedule. But for PIMOs who, to varying degrees, have disconnected the organization's religious rites from their spiritual identity, the demands of WTS are a constant reminder of the precariousness of their position. Every congregation meeting, every hour spent in the door-to-door ministry, every social event organized by the congregation is a potential trauma trigger.

This chapter is a glimpse into the high-demand lifestyle of JWs from the perspective of a PIMO. Below is a sample weekly schedule for a JW. These events are considerably challenging for someone who no longer has intrinsic motivation to attend them. A PIMO is left to balance his or her involvement in these activities in a way that will not arouse suspicion from fellow JWs but that safeguards their personal boundaries, values, and integrity.

• Daily Bible reading—All JWs are expected to have a program of daily personal Bible reading. For those who maintain a flawless commitment to the habit, it contributes to a sense of spiritual superiority. For those who miss a day here or there, it is a constant reminder of their failure to live up to Jehovah's standards. Like an unsuccessful dieter, they set the best of intentions and fizzle out before day twenty-three, only to be reminded again in a particularly motivating talk at the Kingdom Hall to take up the task again. As it is largely unregulated, PIMOs can feel free to give this up. But they best be prepared to answer the interrogations of overly inquisitive elders attempting to assess their spirituality while walking between doors in the proselytizing work: "So what have you been reading lately in your daily Bible reading?"

• JW Broadcasting—If you've never seen one of these, they are worth a watch. They are blatantly propagandist but offer outsiders an incredible view into the bizarre world of WTS. PIMO youths may be subject to a monthly, in-home viewing of this program. But those with more control over their home situation can privately abstain. Again, one must be prepared to avoid conversations that will inevitably arise in JW social settings regarding the latest broadcast to avoid judgment and unwanted attention from the community.

• Meetings—The meetings of JWs consist of a mid-week meeting and a weekend meeting. Each meeting is one and three-quarter hours long. JWs are expected to come early to the meetings and stay late afterward to make the best use of every opportunity to "incite to love and fine works" and "encourage one another" (Hebrews 10:24,25; Watch Tower, 2013a). If a PIMO does not want to incur the prying eyes of the elders and elicit further intrusion into their personal affairs, it is best to comply with this directive to the extent that it is personally tolerable. However, subjection to such forced socialization can be particularly painful for victims of RTS who have yet to develop the skills necessary to set boundaries of intimacy with JW acquaintances. The constant inquiry into personal and emotional well-being may well feel threatening at first. Further, general respect for a person's privacy is not explicitly instructed in JW literature and therefore may be violated by overzealous members.

• Field service—The door-to-door ministry is portrayed as volunteer work in which JWs can choose the extent of their involvement. However, for many years there was an unspoken rule among elders that spiritually healthy publishers should at least meet the "national average" of about ten hours per month. To this day, in some congregations, elders start to get concerned if publishers without extenuating circumstances fall consistently below this metric and may start scheduling personal follow-up calls to encourage greater involvement. To the extent that a PIMO is comfortable fabricating his or her field service report, they can avoid most of this obligation to proselytize. However, since the preaching work is coordinated by the congregation and members are asked to appear at daily kick-off meetings, being less visible in the ministry than your report suggests could prompt elders to pry.

• Conventions and assemblies—These events are meant to be refreshing occasions of spiritual fellowship for JWs. Indeed, for the devout, they are just that. But for the victim of RTS, they may become intense trauma triggers. Conventions and assemblies are chock-full of personal experiences, emotion-laden propaganda videos, and reunions with friends who will inevitably ask personal questions to size up your spirituality for comparison's sake (much like when someone at a cocktail party asks you "What do you do for work?"). Each day of a convention or assembly lasts eight hours. Attendees are asked to stay on campus during lunch to share in spiritual fellowship. It's hard to stomach for PIMOs. In the first few months following the onset of my RTS, I found these events excruciating.

• Elders' meetings—These are, of course, not required for the rank and file. But as it stands, they are still a part of my regular schedule. The elder's manual says that elders are to meet twice a year and that meetings should last no longer than two hours. In many congregations, the elders struggle to meet this time restriction. Meetings may extend well beyond two hours as elders discuss everything from the maintenance of the kingdom hall to recent incidents of inappropriate social media activity by congregation members. My personal goal for each elders' meeting, to the extent possible, is to diplomatically moderate attempts at the coercion of lay witnesses. I try to use thought-provoking vocabulary to unload the language. Duplicitous, I know. And things don't always go my way. Perhaps one day, a conflict of my principles will become unavoidable, and I will be compelled to resign. Until then, I avoid that eventuality, hoping that I might use my position to benefit other PIMOs.

For persons suffering from RTS, religious belief and involvement are their index trauma. Therefore, any of the above events carry the potential to trigger PTSD symptoms including panic attacks, suicidal ideation, and intrusive thoughts. In one family of which I am personally aware, a baptized PIMO son expressed to his parents his intellectual disagreement with WTS. The father demanded that his teenage son continue to attend meetings as long as he was living in the family home. The poor kid had a panic attack at every meeting for months. In my personal experience, congregation meetings had the potential to create significant mental confusion and sharp bursts of anger for up to a year after the onset of my RTS symptoms. Manipulative speech from the platform would send me fuming to the Kingdom Hall parking lot and the safety of my car. I learned quickly to make a point of offering a reassuring smile as I exited the building in response to the prying eyes of congregation elders. This mitigated further suspicion and interrogation. I'm much better now, although congregation meetings are still the most stressful and soul-crushing parts of my week.

Triple-faceted Stigma

In Chapter 4, regarding the stigma facing homosexual JWs, I quoted Lalich & McLaren's research from their 2010 article "Inside and Outcast: Multifaceted Stigma and Redemption in the Lives of Gay and Lesbian Jehovah's Witnesses" (Lalich & McLaren, 2010). In this section, as Lalich & McLaren did for homosexual JWs, I will apply the framework for stigma outlined in Erving Goffman's 1963 publication *Stigma: Notes on the Management of Spoiled Identity* (Goffman, 1963) to PIMOs. As it is for LGBTQ+ JWs, triple-faceted stigma is an everyday reality for PIMOs whose silent stigma is based on intellectual dissent.

According to Goffman, stigma is "the situation of the individual who is disqualified from full social acceptance" (Goffman, 2009, p. 3). Of course, the stigma of disfellowshipped and disassociated JWs is explicit. They are formally rejected from the community and shunned by relatives and friends. However, Goffman also draws attention to a different kind of stigma that affects individuals who, although not overtly *discredited*, are *discreditable* by way of a secret disqualifier undisclosed to the community. The PIMO who chooses to maintain intellectual opposition and psychological independence from WTS harbors an undisclosed secret that, if exposed, would lead to their rejection. An ever-present potential exists for the PIMO to be reduced by their community "from a whole and usual person to a tainted, discounted one" (Goffman, 1963, p. 3). In the JW world, the PIMO could be exposed as a non-supporter of the WTS mission, an apostate no longer favored by God and under the influence of Satan the Devil.

As Lalich & McLaren highlight, "having set itself apart from mainstream society, in many respects the Witness world serves as the dominant culture for active members." Thus, JWs who face stigma within their religious community must deal "without a sense of integration on at least two levels." On the outside, they are stigmatized for being religious fundamentalists. On the inside, they are stigmatized for their inability to feel the same uncritical enthusiasm for the wonderfulness of WTS that is the hallmark of their spiritual brethren.

Prior to disillusionment, the devout JW can escape stigmatization from outsiders by means of comradery with their spiritual brotherhood. Many JWs feel that they are indeed at home with their spiritual family when they attend their weekly Kingdom Hall meetings, finally safe from the dangers of the outside world. However, the PIMO, still battling her neurological fear response to the outside world, no longer experiences safety within the spiritual community. Instead, the spiritual community represents an additional threat of social rejection.

What makes the stigma triple-faceted is the PIMO's internal stigmatization of themselves. The entrance of critical cognition into consciousness is at first interpreted by the burgeoning PIMO as spiritual weakness, uncleanness, or apostasy. WTS admits that some JWs might find new doctrine or procedures implemented by the Faithful & Discreet Slave difficult to accept at first. But the ability to bring "every thought into captivity to make it obedient to Christ" (2 Corinthians 10:4; Watch Tower, 2013a) is considered evidence of one's spiritual maturity and humility. As discussed in previous chapters, this psychological battle of repressing dissenting thoughts and attitudes is destructive and may lead to mental anguish in the form of depression and anxiety.

Triple-faceted stigma is overwhelming. It requires PIMOs to simultaneously defend themselves against the dangers of an unknown world of non-witnesses, the disciplinary action of the elders and self-policing lay-witnesses, and their own automatic thoughts of self-condemnation.

This pressure is reason enough for many PIMOs to make the painfully difficult and permanent decision to disassociate themselves from the organization. Many find relief and acceptance with communities of fellow ex-members. This is an understandable decision. However, the PIMO who chooses to remain must develop the skills necessary to maintain psychological stability knowing full well that they are "discreditable" within the community. This ability to self-present in a way that prevents ostracism by a social group is referred to as the control of social information (Goffman, 1963). More on the PIMO superpower of social information control and its implications for greater society in the final chapter.

In the meantime, triple-faceted stigma is a day-to-day reality for PIMOs, particularly ones who live in a home with other devout witnesses or those who otherwise have very little control over their freedoms. Every meeting, every hour in the field ministry, every family worship with believing parents or husbands, is a reckoning with the ever-present reality of their newly acquired stigma.

> 1/17/19
>
> It's incredible how the tables turn on you in this organization. It's a brotherhood alright. But if you think differently or act differently, they'll turn on you in a heartbeat. Heck, even your family will turn on you.
>
> I feel like somehow I have lost their trust. Witnesses think that a person's goodness can be measured by how much theocratic work they are doing. If you go the opposite way on the theocratic work-o-meter, distrust mounts.

As an example of rhetoric promoting a quick rejection of the disloyal, notice the quote below discussed at the Kingdom Hall, from a recent issue of *Watchtower*. The circumstances of this anecdote sounded very similar to my own.

> Jehovah will patiently wait until the end of the thousand years before he expects us to be perfect. Until that time, Jehovah is willing to overlook our sins (…) Consider the example of one sister whose husband began suffering from severe anxiety attacks and stopped attending meetings. "This was very painful for me," she says. "Our plans for our

> future as a family were turned upside down." Yet through it all, this loving wife was patient with her husband. She relied on Jehovah and never gave up. Like Jehovah, she looked past the problem and focused on the good things about her husband. (Watch Tower, 2020c, p. 19)

In the above passage, panic attacks are connected to imperfection and sin. It is suggested that the wife overlook the problem by focusing on the husband's good qualities and acquiring patience. As a member of the congregation who had endured this very experience, I interpreted this account as a classic example of RTS in the JW community. The man with social anxiety and panic attacks is quickly stigmatized. He is referred to only as the loyal sister's husband and not as a "brother" himself.

3/10/19

> It takes everything out of me just to be around people. It feels crazy sometimes. How did I ever do it before? Or is it still that I am internalizing some insecurity? I could be so easily rejected by anyone in "The Truth". The people with whom I have been as open as possible about my feelings and lifestyle still end the conversation with "as long as you are faithful to Jehovah."

While the PIMO is facing the struggles inherent to the culture of the community, they simultaneously face the challenge of reconstruction; the task of anyone who leaves totalist ideology. They must recreate their morals, values, and cognitive constructs in the absence of WTS doctrine. But reconstruction is not limited to matters of faith and morality. It includes reconstructing professional and career pursuits, redefining friendship and family relationships, and planning for a future that was never supposed to happen. People generally base their goals and aspirations upon a set of underlying values that they have shaped over many years of psychological development. However, in the early stages of RTS, all such values are nonexistent. All previous concepts of faith, motivation, morality, and principles were connected to the theology that has been lost.

RTS victims in general may pass through this inferno with the support of a therapist or support group. Uniquely though, PIMOs may be left to navigate this terrifying phase alone. Family and friends cannot bear to hear the PIMO's blasphemous speech. In their fear of losing their loved one to apostasy, they desperately call for the help of congregation elders. Thus, the PIMO's most intimate human connections become the very enforcers of the traumatizing environment. This isolation may be exacerbated by the PIMO's residual fear of mental health practitioners. WTS has encouraged skepticism of psychotherapy for many years because of the challenges it can present to faith (Watch Tower, 1981). Professional mental health support was considered a last option, not the first. By the time PIMOs with RTS seek mental health support, they may already have been subjected to several coercive and triggering visits by congregation elders in their very home, reminding the victim of how rebellious and worthy of death they would be if they chose to leave the organization.

PIMOs are fearful of friends and family who can betray them to the elders. And they are afraid to speak with anyone outside of the organization for fear that the outsider might unravel whatever thread of faith remains for them to cling to. They are in a prison of internal and external fear.

Career and Education

Victims of RTS may find themselves unprepared for work in the professional sphere. JWs indeed have jobs; some even in the professional sphere. But many JWs work for themselves or at small part-time jobs that do not require post-secondary education. Additionally, many have given up their financial independence in favor of full-time volunteer assignments with the organization. Some have served at Bethel headquarters for decades; others as missionaries on a small stipend from the organization. If compelled to discontinue their assignments, they are left with no education or work history with which to reconstruct a sustainable means of income. While not overtly discouraged, the common concern of retirement planning is rarely mentioned in WTS literature. Basing one's decisions on the stalwart belief that God's final war at Armageddon is imminent can foster financial unpreparedness for the future.

I quickly came to realize that I was relying on the JW community to provide for some of my most basic material necessities. Awakening to the fact that not only my social network but also my means of sustenance could evaporate if I ever divulged my ethical disagreement with WTS was trauma upon trauma. At the time, I was renting from a landlord who provided me with a reduced rate because of my position in the organization. With my theocratic status gone, my rate would double in a matter of months. The meager income I used to pay my reduced rent came from a job with a JW employer. As questions in the community arose about my reduced involvement in oversight and evangelical activities, so did the pressure for an explanation at work. Both my housing and my income were in jeopardy.

Relationships

1/19/19

Sometimes I wish it would go away. I wish I could be an elder and join in. I wish people would respect me and understand how hard the past year has been. When people in the congregation encourage me to take on more responsibility it seems like they are saying: "I know you are happy now and theocratic service made you suicidally depressed and miserable. But we'd really like you to do it again and be a little more miserable please."

I suppose they mean: "I'm still nervous that you are in a bad place with God. We want you to thrive again. The only way we know for sure that someone is 'doing good in the truth' is to see them move up the hierarchy of the organization."

12/16/18

> I want so badly to stay with my wife. I don't want to grow out of love with her. Our work with the organization was a common goal that drew us together. It may not have been healthy, but it sure did make us a team. With that gone I don't know how we are going to connect.

Establishing and re-establishing relationships is an immense challenge to the PIMO. The most binding element in all their relationships has now evaporated. JWs view marriage as a spiritual union. For this reason, they are only allowed to marry "in the Lord." A married couple is described as a three-fold cord with God; a rope of three intertwined cords that draw strength from each other and become unbreakable. As the song often sung at the Kingdom Hall says, "when God is in a marriage, then problems will be few." (Watch Tower, *Sing Praises*). But what about when God is not in a marriage? If the blossoming PIMO divulges their doubts, the believing mate might begin to see them as a threat to their faith. This can lead to a distancing both emotionally and intimately. As I mentioned earlier, the believing JW might desperately call upon the elders to rid the awakening PIMO of his doubts. This is a threatening insertion of the organization into the marital union. The disillusioned PIMO may fear that the loyalty of their closest friend and romantic partner is not to them, but the organization. The devout JW spouse might even repeat the incriminating comments of the PIMO to the elders, further arousing their suspicion and perhaps even judicial action. Thus, the PIMO may be forced into a period of silence if he or she chooses to remain in the marriage.

From accounts provided of disillusioned JWs online, it appears that some marriages do not make it past this troubling time. Divorce may result as a couple realizes, with years of marriage behind them, that they suddenly seem to have very little in common. Households may become thick with distrust. The religious conflict may be unbearable. With this breakdown comes the opportunity for the other party to develop extramarital sexual intimacy thus forcing a disfellowshipping and the end of the marriage.

WTS has blamed the breakup of families and marriages on non-witnesses who refuse to accept the newfound beliefs of a newly baptized JW (Watch Tower, 2020d). No doubt this is the case at times. At other times, however, it is the JW family who refuses to adjust to the newfound beliefs of their PIMO family member. If a marriage stays together after one spouse's disillusionment, the believing spouse is encouraged to follow the counsel found in the Bible book of Peter to attempt to win over unbelievers "without a word" to the faith (1 Peter 3:1, Watch Tower, 2013a). Success stories are repeated in *Watchtower* articles to keep the hopes and efforts of the believing spouse up. Despite years of union, the JW couple may not have the requisite skills to reconcile their moral, ethical, ideological, and political differences, skills that are common in many happy marriages and civil unions among outsiders.

1/20/19

One flesh. Jehovah's Witnesses interpret that scripture to mean that we have to do everything together. That two people have identical faith and moral leanings. That's not expressly in the verse (even if it were, it wouldn't matter). It's just that we've seen hours of video drilling it into our brains. Happy couples doing door-to-door ministry together.

It's true that there are natural things that a husband and wife will team up on. Creating a safe and comforting home. Having children. But to say they have to be identical is ridiculous. For the first time in a long time, I have some individuality and personal goals. At home, we laugh and joke, and we are happy. Then when we go to the meeting... depressed, sad, guilty.

The Psycho-Spiritual Journey

The onset of RTS was the first phase in an ongoing journey of deconstructing beliefs and biases that I had held my entire life and a re-evaluation of my every assumption of truth. The source of all knowledge and wisdom, trumping anything to the contrary that I had ever heard from "spiritually weak" witnesses and non-witnesses alike, was the *New World Translation of the Holy Scriptures* and everything published by WTS in written, audio, or video format. I was raised on WTS children's books; the infamous *My Book of Bible Stories* that was read at bedtime to many JW children of my generation. (More recently, children of JW parents watch the animated series *Become Jehovah's Friend* in which Caleb and Sophia, children of JW parents, teach moral lessons ranging from avoiding superhero movies to the immorality of homosexuality.) All learning from public primary school was passed through the filter of the "sacred science." Given that all of my thinking was aligned with the rhetoric of an organization that I now deemed to be untrustworthy, I was left questioning everything that I had ever known.

The dissolution of all thought into blank consciousness is not uncommon for the practitioner of Eastern mindfulness pursuits. While the feeling can be uncomfortable at first, it comes to be a familiar experience that is ubiquitous to all moments of life, like a peaceful stream trickling quietly beneath the raging currents of emotional and cognitive experience. Accepting that all previously held beliefs are illusory, meaningless, and deconstructable at any moment leaves one with a calmness of experience that is ever-present and parallel to all states of mind, including joy and suffering. As I released myself from the manipulative grip of my beliefs and social environment, I began to taste this unaffected mental state for the very first time. It was psychological liberty.

I understand that I must use the term "spirituality" with caution. Its meaning is subject largely to the cultural interpretation and life experience of each reader. Our perception of spirituality is formed by our religious beliefs, whether explicit or implicit, and by infinite variations in human psychological experience. To a JW, spirituality is correlated with the inner acceptance of WTS doctrine and the extent of one's performance of theocratic tasks. Disillusioned JWs face the challenge of reclaiming ownership of spirituality from the corporation that previously usurped it.

For the time being, I prefer Carl Sagan's definition of spirituality:

> When we recognize our place in an immensity of light years and the passage of ages, when we grasp the intricacy, beauty and subtlety of life, then that soaring feeling, that sense of elation and humility combined, is surely spiritual (Sagan, 2011)

The quest to experience and maintain delicate harmony with this state in everyday life is what I shall call, for the purposes of this book, my spiritual journey. Such a spiritual quest does not depend on a system of beliefs, acceptance of any doctrine, or association with any religious group. It does not require theism or adamant atheism. It is the journey of all humankind, not just those recovering from religious trauma. It is the worthy work of a lifetime full of curiosity and exploration. For most people, the spiritual journey takes place in concurrently with psychological maturation, in fits and spurts across the lifespan. The victim of RTS, on the other hand, accelerates through much of this journey all at once, in a matter of moments, and must put forth much effort to alight upon a stable velocity of spiritual journeying that can be maintained in the long term.

A crucial step in the spiritual journey is the deconstruction of the entity Jehovah. WTS encourages JWs to place their relationship with Jehovah in the position of highest priority in their lives. Jehovah is connected to all daily activities. Prayer to Jehovah opens and closes each day. It is a self-performed bedtime story each evening, assuring the true believer that everything is in God's hands and that all is right with the world. As I have previously mentioned, deconstruction of the personage Jehovah was by far the most traumatic of my entire RTS experience. This is likely the case for many former JWs. Some who were involved religiously before their conversion to WTS may have a pre-existing psychological concept of God to which they may revert. If, for example, someone was from a sect of Protestantism before baptism as a JW, one may still cling to the traditional God of the New Testament and take comfort in childhood constructs of a loving God. But for JWs who were "raised in the truth", the only concept of God that to which they have ever subscribed is that of the WTS-owned God, Jehovah. It is no wonder then that many disillusioned JWs claim atheism and agnosticism upon distancing themselves from the organization.

As for me, I knew that transcending trauma required forgiveness. So, I had to forgive Jehovah for his contribution to my trauma. If the universe was indeed of His deliberate construction, it was full of design flaws. It appeared for the first time that Jehovah was not as limitlessly wise as I had imagined. Perhaps he set a process in motion that he was powerless to control. Regardless, prior to my acceptance of the possible nonexistence of God, I had to reckon with the fact that it was Jehovah who was responsible for evil; all the evils of the world across the millennia. More personally, Jehovah was going to let my beloved wife die one day. I was justifiably angry. I cursed Him. And then I forgave Him.

2/21/19

I don't get this part. Why did The Creator make us just to die? Maybe that was the best he could do.

> Thank you anyway. I still love it. I still love life. Thank you. It's okay. You did the best you could. I forgive you. It's beautiful.

While releasing oneself from accountability to a higher power is liberating, the process is a rocky one. As Lifton puts it, "cultism—like all totalism and fundamentalism—is a reaction against the potential confusion of protean openness" (Lifton, 2019, p.12). The belief in a doctrine that supplies the answers to all of life's biggest questions provides a feeling (albeit illusory) of safety in an entropic universe. With this psychological safeguard gone, the RTS sufferer is not only dealing with the grief of losing their best friend, father, provider, and savior, they are also losing the childlike comfort that comes from unquestionably following such a perfect leader. With the death of their supreme judge and law-giver, the newly liberated agnostic or atheist must for the first time in their life learn to govern and comfort themselves.

> 3/15/19

> I have to reconstruct my psyche at the deepest levels. At a time when I know nothing, I have to observe the world around me and reconstruct a doctrine based only on information I have at the moment and anything else I might have read up until now.

> Still, I am attacked. Nobody in my life can acknowledge that I have been wronged by the organization. Not even my family when I am literally bawling my eyes out about the injustice done to

me. Meanwhile, we cry at every meeting; fine every other time of the week; bawling at the meeting.

Still, I'm in the wrong?! How does that work exactly? I suppose I just want to be heard. Everyone is too afraid to console me.

The second task for the PIMO is to build a set of values from scratch. Most people undergo the construction of values based on input from disparate sources and in phases across the lifespan. For example, as a homework assignment to help clients identify their personal values, some psychotherapists ask their clients to list the values of their mother in one column and the values of their father in a second. In a third column, the assignment is to list their own values: some sort of fusion of the two combined with personal learning and experience. But what happens when Mom and Dad's values and all personal experience align with the values of an organization that you no longer trust? What remains is a blank third column and the overwhelming task of analyzing every information source all at once; fragments of truth exploding like shrapnel from a hand grenade in the direction of your intellect. It is unfortunate that in this naivete, the ex-JW is susceptible to manipulation by charismatic leaders of all sorts and is at risk of getting swept up with another influential community at the expense of developing a balanced individual perspective.

In normal psychological development, the teenage years are a time of rebellion. Teenagers challenge familial and cultural norms and begin establishing new ones based on personal perspectives and those of their peers.

While teenage rebellion does prune away from WTS many teenage children of JW adults, the process can lead to radicalization in others. Although they do not dare articulate this overtly, JW parents may well have moderated their application of WTS mores and display a degree of deviance from the rhetoric to which they have been subjecting their children at weekly congregation meetings. Therefore, some rebellious JW teens frame the moderation that their parents have acquired over decades in the organization as hypocrisy and turn inwardly into the idealism of the theology. Something similar was seen from 2014 to 2016 as children of relatively moderate Islamic parents were wooed by the scriptural idealism of the Islamic State's recruitment efforts. Similarly, a JW teen's rejection of social norms and construction of personal values can lead them to an even more fervent commitment to WTS. Given WTS's stance on higher education, JW children do not experience the coming-of-age rituals that many American children experience while attending colleges and universities and being exposed to new opinions and intellectual perspectives.

Another step in the spiritual journey is tied to sexuality. With biblical and organizational standards for sexual morality out of the way, one must reframe opinions regarding sexual orientation, gender expression, and the meaning of the marital or monogamous union. Western culture has made considerable progress in awareness of the spectrum of sexual and gender expression. The PIMO is now faced with the challenge of determining their personal stance on matters of sexuality while battling the programmed emotional responses of guilt and fear triggered by unsanctioned sexual practices. Some PIMOs no doubt find that the marital commitments they made in their ignorance must be re-evaluated.

An ongoing phase of the spiritual journey includes simultaneous harnessing and deconstructing of the concepts of self and ego. The spiritual process of liberation from the egoic self is a transcendental one. However, this must not be confused with the doctrine expounded in the Holy Bible of "considering that others are superior to you" (Philippians 2:3; Watch Tower, 2013a). Although the process of reducing the effects of an arrogant ego is mentioned heavily in Watch Tower literature, it is encouraged at the expense of personal recognition of intellectual ability and creative talents. Thus, the PIMO may struggle to honor their individuality, self-knowledge, and healthy pride. When independent thinking, opinion, and interpretation conflict with WTS teaching, JWs are warned of the dangers of indulging:

> In modern times, a very small number among God's people have become disgruntled with some aspect of Christian teaching and have murmured against the earthly part of Jehovah's organization. Why does this happen? (…) Pride may play a role, and some fall into the trap of independent thinking. Whatever the reason, such murmuring is hazardous, since it can draw us back into the world and its ways. (Watch Tower, 2006, p. 22)

The mutual task of strengthening individual vision and potential while avoiding egoism is a challenge for the PIMO. All while getting regular doses of self-denying rhetoric at the meetings.

I hope that this chapter sheds some light on a sociological phenomenon that goes largely undiscussed in the academic literature about WTS and other NRMs. I also hope that my personal experience as a PIMO may bring comfort to others in this complex situation. It is time to bring more awareness to the PIMO phenomenon and the organizational policies that lead to its occurrence. Although this group is a small subset within a small subset of society at large, their stories deserve to be told and their rights and freedoms deserve to be protected.

8. Transcending Ideological Dogma in the Broader Community

3/3/19

I'm a damn lucky man. Every time I try to hate Jehovah's Witnesses too much, I remember that they made my wife who she is today.

Hell, in a way they made me me.

Or at least they certainly helped make us us.

Even if we have out-grown it.

There is a fascination with cults not only in the social sciences but also in the general population, largely because they exist as extreme manifestations of ubiquitous principles of social psychology. For social scientists, cults are intriguing case studies. For the general population, titillating voyeurism of the dangers of losing objectivity. Journalistic exposés of cults proliferate in made-for-streaming documentaries. These programs are the sociological equivalent of serial killer documentaries. American viewers love this stuff.

In response to popular media about cult-like groups, there is a tendency toward a different kind of "thought-terminating cliché" from outsiders. Viewers tell each other with a shivering spookiness usually reserved for ghost stories that "It could happen to any one of us." Then, they go about their business thinking that as long as they don't encounter a wide-eyed disciple of Do and Ti, they are safe from cult indoctrination and brainwashing.

The reality is that as social primates, *Homo sapiens* are constantly at risk of losing objectivity in the flow of social interaction. We are biologically predisposed to organizing ourselves in tribes and communities. We could remove ourselves from all social influence, but only at the expense of all social connection. Therefore, to the extent that each of us develops relationships with fellow humans, we are opening ourselves up to the possibility of social influence and thought conformity.

The last five to ten years of US political debate have shown the glaring repercussions of extreme social influence and polarization of thought. We are experiencing the death of the center. Social media silos result in the complete absorption of individuals into an environment of one-sided ideology. Compounding the problem, social networks use algorithms to extend a user's time on the platform; delivering more and more content that reaffirms the user's ideological persuasions. The resulting psychosocial climate edges dangerously close to that of closed religious communities like WTS. Without regular exposure to dissenting voices, the opinions of like-minded cohorts become more and more extreme. This is a phenomenon that psychologists refer to as social polarization.

Do you actively follow social media pages from your political and ideological opponents, not as a refuel for antagonistic debate, but in an effort to understand the thinking of the out-group and balance your own belief systems? If not, you could be at risk of social polarization; the radicalization of your views over time that results from limiting your association to people who share your same viewpoint; be it in political, religious, or ethical matters.

Of course, beyond social media silos, totalist communities exist in the real world too. I will discuss just two such communities that show marked similarities to my own.

For one, Islamic immigrant populations challenged with integrating with Western society face similar pivotal moments and decisions to those that fell upon the early Bible Students movement discussed in Chapter 2—the decision, when met with social friction, to either integrate or radicalize. I suspect that within such communities, many will suffer RTS upon awakening to the conflict between certain fundamental principles of their faith and the humanism of the West. Disillusioned Muslims may suffer significant spiritual guilt and moral injury PTSD for proliferating damaging doctrine as do disillusioned JWs.

A second group includes the fundamentalist Christian communities of the American South where religious opposition to the LGBTQ+ community continues. Teenagers who endeavor to explore their sexuality regularly hear homophobic comments from their parents despite the progress in Western culture and the introduction of alternative viewpoints in entertainment, literature, and the like. They experience tremendous anxiety at the thought of openly articulating their sexuality or gender identity and incurring the disapproval of their parents, or worse, alienation from supportive family relationships. In some cases, this is exactly what happens. Although the LGBTQ+ community and its supporters would happily embrace the socially rejected, the finality of such an ignominious exit from family and one's community of upbringing is nonetheless traumatic. To the extent that connection with genetically similar family is conducive to long-term psychological well-being, the loss of such connections can create gaps that even the most well-meaning non-family support systems may struggle to fill. Not only the one who exits the totalist community, but also those who remain suffer from the separation.

Some sources of influence are significantly more persuasive than others and carry big sticks. Among these are nation-states, advertising campaigns, and toxic relationships; all of them bidding for the allegiance of our minds. Egoic fantasies further muddy the waters of rational thinking and psychological independence. So while many of my readers have no connection to the above communities or with a totalist NRM environment, that does not mean that they are immune to the dangers of undue social influence.

In my quest for psychological freedom within a captive organization, I have learned lessons that apply well beyond the small subset of disillusioned JWs that is the focus of this book. I will discuss a few of these lessons in this chapter. I do not intend to be prescriptive in the following discussion. For true therapeutic support in the spiritual journey away from damaging religion, I suggest reading *Leaving the Fold* by Dr. Winell written specifically to help those who have negative experiences with religion and to provide them with some guidance moving forward. Also, find a licensed psychotherapist; preferably one with experience treating RTS.

As a JW elder with a rich experience manipulating the thinking of my fellow man often to less than optimal outcomes, I will modestly bow out from offering advice. I have a deep-seated fear of my capacity to cause significant psychological damage by offering ill-advised spiritual direction. And I am not a psychotherapist. However, I will share the steps that led me to acquire what I shall call my PIMO superpowers. Others in PIMO-like situations may be able to draw some comparisons to their circumstances and find some benefit.

To be clear, I cannot recommend that any JW, or others in PIMO-like circumstances, remain to the point of serious psychological harm. But the reality is that some will choose to maintain such a tenuous balance for a time, to affect a different outcome than permanent ostracization from their community.

Temporarily, this is my situation. For those who might be interested, here's what has helped me.

Mindfulness and Reverse Engineering Lifton's Criteria

Reverse engineering Lifton's criteria of thought reform provides a mechanism with which to analyze one's faulty cognition. The PIMO, still subject to propagandist rhetorical and social pressure from WTS, has ample opportunity to mindfully observe the reactions of their mind to these coercive stimuli. Mindfulness meditation trains an individual's ability to challenge emotion-based or distorted beliefs. Regular meditation practice enables a practitioner to attain a sort of distance from his mind – a distance that allows him to note sensation, thought and emotion as an observer rather than identifying personally with the experience as many humans appear to do.

PTSD research has identified an interesting neurological finding about the speed with which the limbic and cortical systems react to emotional stimuli. The limbic system is much quicker. Therefore, the overwhelming affective sensations of trauma, and programmed emotional reactions such as fear and excitement, repeat in awareness even after an individual has cognitively deconstructed the irrational belief systems underpinning the emotional sensations. For example, a PIMO may know intellectually that the body of knowledge from science and academia is not a pack of lies designed by a supernatural wicked spirit creature to turn them against Jehovah. However, they could still experience a programmed fear response when reading such material.

It is the work of the mindfulness meditator to differentiate the ABCs of psychology: affect (emotional sensation), behavior (reactions to thoughts and feelings), and cognition (thoughts). The ability to parse disparate elements of conscious experience allows mindfulness practitioners to identify clearly when affect and behavior are being activated by emotion-laden rhetoric or social influence. Instead of immediately accepting the automated responses of affect, behavior, and cognition, the skilled meditator can hit the pause button and make pragmatic behavioral decisions. The PIMO does well to develop this skill. This psychological strength allows one to identify any improper influence whether it emanates from a social group, advertisers, toxic family members, or ideologically polarizing rhetoric.

Of course, even well-meaning people use emotion to motivate. Parents of young children have very little other option. Emotions have their place making our lives beautiful, but they can be used against us. Caution must be paid to any intellectual stance arising in consciousness that is strongly connected to an emotional sensation. The better we get at identifying and challenging our automatic behavioral and cognitive reactions to emotional experience, the more we will succeed in creating social frameworks, businesses, organizations, and political movements that bring the most benefit to the most people and the future of humanity as a whole.

That being said, it may also be the case that, upon analysis of consciousness, the emotionally conditioned response *is* the most effective. So while meditating, a PIMO may discover that an element of their emotional programming is not actually to their detriment or to that of others. An indoctrinated belief or behavior is not categorically flawed just because it is proliferated by an NRM. The strong reactive psychological state of the betrayed RTS victim described in Chapter 5 must be moderated so as not to automatically reject earlier conclusions simply because of a visceral rejection of everything they learned from WTS, their spiritual abuser.

Lifton's eight criteria are red flags to prompt deeper personal analysis. If in consciousness, a belief or behavior appears connected to one of Lifton's criteria, it must be re-examined. Does the automatic thought result from your restrictive social environment (milieu control), the emotional connotation of a particular word or phrase (loading the language), belief in the supernatural (mystic manipulation, sacred science), or an illusory standard for human goodness (demand for purity)? If so, hold the thought in your awareness for a time. Analyze it. Ask yourself what flavor or essence the thought has. Then determine if this essence is based on evidential data or an ideological bias.

When the above steps are followed, a process ensues of an increasingly nuanced and complex worldview wherein the psychological fabric created by the totalist environment gradually disintegrates. The result is the bifurcation of thought towards fresh and creative cognition, releasing you from the psychological captivity of a traumatic religious upbringing.

For a JW, an important question to ask oneself as they deconstruct the effects of coercive persuasion is: "If Jehovah told the Faithful & Discreet Slave tomorrow to end the disfellowshipping policy, how would I respond?" (dispensing of existence, doctrine over person). "If there were no threat of losing my family and friends forever, what would I do?" When meditating, it is also important to identify what the compulsion to confess feels like and then isolate and label the sensation. The process of dialing down intimacy with congregation elders can be heart-wrenching, but it may well provide the opportunity to analyze when you feel compelled to share private information that one would much rather keep private (cult of confession).

The result of this process can be what WTS refers to as a "double life" (indicating deceitful hypocrisy on the part of entrapped members) or what Lifton calls the "protean self" (Lifton, 2019). The concept of the protean self is named after a shape-shifting character from Greek mythology. Lifton prescribes the protean approach as "a view of the self as always in process; as being many-sided rather than monolithic, and resilient rather than fixed" (Lifton, 2019, p.63). The protean self is "characterized by openness, change, and new beginnings, and strongly resists the ownership by others" (Lifton, 2019, p.63). It is strategic in its use of conformity; bending aspects of its self-presentation to fit the norms of multiple groups at the same, all the while refusing to compromise independent thought. The protean person can do this within multiple communities to accomplish mutual goals without submitting to any group's ideology at the deepest levels of their psyche. To a PIMO, self-presenting strategically in a calculated effort to convince various social audiences of allegiance with surface-deep displays of comradery might seem disingenuous, underhanded, or political at first; but it is empowering and may allow them to construct a place of psychological refuge from the constant barrage of pressure to conform from congregation elders, lay-witnesses and WTS rhetoric.

In *The Evolving Self: A Psychology for the Third Millennium*, Mihaly Csikszentmihalyi describes the upward spiral of an individual's evolution toward self-actualization. The upward spiral consists of phases of individualization and integration. Victims of RTS perform a dramatic version of this process. Their initial individualization separates them from their religious communities bringing the onset of

RTS. The disillusioned religionist must then confront the challenge of individualizing from ideological totalism and integrating with the larger community, while simultaneously integrating in a more balanced and sustainable way with precious relationships they desire to maintain inside the totalist community. This turbulent process can be the path to stable dissent that protects friendships from unnecessary damage. In the case of disillusioned JWs who choose to remain in the organization, individualization can progress in phases punctuated by reintegration with JWs, ex-JWs, and non-JWs based on what feels appropriate to the PIMO. Approaching dissent in this way can facilitate a cooling of the inferno of RTS without softening the PIMO's newfound principles and values.

For many, the complete actualization of the self may eventually require formal expulsion from the group. Further, the challenge described above of maintaining psychological independence while still subject to WTS policies would be a non-issue if the organization ended disfellowshipping, disassociation, and enforced shunning.

3/17/19

I have learned not to model myself after anyone. But to identify the good and bad in everyone and learn from both. Also, I have to identify the bad in JWs and somehow not judge them for contributing to a harmful arrangement.

It's not easy.

I'm creating a new kind of love.

The Unsung Superpower of Minority Influence

Being PIMO takes a lot of courage. In my case, as an elder who seeks to moderate the abuses of the organization, I must regularly stand up against deeply inculcated fears that have been inculcated in me by the organization since my youth. I have learned that my deepest subconscious fears are just toothless tigers. I have also had to reckon with some painful existential realities. Among these: eternal nonexistence after death, godlessness, my potential for great evil, and the meaninglessness of life. Fear of prosecution by the organization for my thought crimes is gradually subsiding from an all-out flood of paranoia to an occasional trickling of nervousness. It helps to know that there are others like me. Although I have never met them, I know that I am in the company of countless PIMOs who refuse to sacrifice their familial relationships to the organization.

In the meantime, I have learned that the silent dissent of PIMOs may have a quantifiable social power. Let me explain.

Famously, Solomon Asch's research in the 1950s quantified the ubiquitous power of majority influence and conformity. In his experiments, subjects were shown two cards with lines printed on them. On one card, a reference line. On the second card, three other lines of varying lengths. Researchers asked the subjects to determine which of the three lines on the second card was the same length as the reference line on the first card. The correct answer was obvious. However, when Asch introduced actors into the research room who deliberately chose the incorrect answer, the results were astounding. The research subject changed his answer to the obviously incorrect answer given by the actors. As the number of actors increased, the more likely it became that the subject would neglect his assessment of reality and conform to the incorrect response of the majority. Asch's experiments provided evidence of the weakness of the untrained human psyche against the pressures of social influence.

But Asch's experiments on majority influence also yielded some subtle and interesting findings about the ability of minority dissenters to effect change within a majority community. When some of the participants stubbornly refused to question themselves, they ended up influencing the majority to alter their viewpoints. These findings were not the focus of the research and largely went unexplored in the literature. It was not until the late 1960s that the French social psychologist Serge Moscovici devoted his efforts to uncovering the mysteries of minority influence.

In the fascinating Blue-Green Studies performed in 1980, Moscovici and his team reversed Asch's majority studies. Instead of filling the research room with actors, they used only one. Then they filled the room with study participants. The researchers projected a series of obviously blue slides in front of the group. The actor then publicly and confidently asserted that the slide was green. Nothing remarkable happened. For the most part, the majority stuck to their guns. They said that the blue slide was blue.

But Moscovici wanted to determine if there was any residual effect of the minority actor's determined confidence on the viewpoint of the subjects. Moscovici believed that individuals experience an authentic conversion of viewpoint as "a means of resolving conflict which has been internalised." He designed the experiment to test this theory using the optical phenomenon of chromatic afterimages. He writes in *Innovation and Minority Influence*:

> We know that if an individual fixates on a white screen after having fixated for a few seconds on a particular colour, he will see the complementary colour on the screen. In this case the relevant complementary colours were yellow-orange (for blue) and red-purple (for green). (Moscovici, 1985, p. 36)

Amazingly, Moscovici found that subjects exposed to the minority influencer experienced an increase in red-purple responses to the afterimage. While they initially rejected the incorrect assertions of the actor that the blue slide was green, the confidence of the actor's response caused them to question themselves in private sometime after they gave their initial response. There was a "hidden influence of which the subjects were not aware" (Moscovici, 1985, p. 36). Moscovici and his team had alighted on the power of minority influence. Moscovici sums it up as follows:

> When each member of the majority finds himself confronted with the same object alone, he perceives and judges it in a way that is closer to the minority point of view. It appears, in other words, that his own point of view is modified without him being conscious of it. (Moscovici, 1985, p. 33)

There you have it, the antidote to harmful majority influence. In the case of Moscovici's studies, the minority was able to affect an authentic inner conversion in the viewpoint of the majority to their obviously incorrect assertion. Moscovici's studies showed that minority influence does not have the same dramatic effects that majority influence does. It was much less pronounced. But minority influence nonetheless had the power to affect inner change in members of the majority. When asked what color afterimage they saw on the white screen, majority members gave the response that corresponded to the minority actor's response. Sometime between their initial response and the afterimage test, they questioned their reality and conformed, at least in part, to the minority view.

Imagine if the majority's opinions were out of harmony with demonstrable facts as a result of social polarization. What if some of the majority participants already harbored secret doubts about the stance of the group of which they were part? How much more of an influence could a minority dissenter have upon the majority if the minority opinion were objectively stronger?

Of course, such dissent could not be that of "rigidity, of 'consistency carried to extremes'" in evidence of a "one-sided determination to influence" and a "clear and blatant refusal to piece together any negotiation" or compromise with the majority (Moscovici, 1985, p. 114). No, this is the path of the minority innovator who seeks to expand the viewpoint of the majority to new possibilities and perspectives. It is the path of the resolute PIMO who determines not to flee from conflict but to take upon herself the personal responsibility of moderating a community. Moscovici describes this as confident consistency in the face of threats of exclusion for standing one's ground.

I have just given you, and any future enemies, the secret to my PIMO superpowers. Please use them responsibly.

I cannot help but think about how beneficial this approach could be for minority groups in many social settings who attempt to undermine the institutional or legislated inequities of earlier generations. I wish that, in the era of polarized political rhetoric and unfiltered opinions on social media, some would instead opt for the much less aggressive approach of the minority influencer. But frankly, it is incredibly difficult. It means placing yourself in the midst of a group that proliferates ideology that you do not support, refusing to remove oneself or to step aside, and playing the strategic game of calculated protean conformity to convince the group of your allegiance. All-the-while harboring the undisclosed goal of affecting genuine internal change in individual members of the majority group.

Welcome to my life as a PIMO minority influencer.

Concluding Comments

Until substantial policy change occurs within WTS, the life-out-loud expressive culture common in recent decades will not be accessible for the PIMO. I am resigned to this for now. It is my decision. I neither defend nor recommend it. But until WTS releases their psychological grip on the people that I love, we are at a stalemate.

Human society constantly strives towards progress. Science and technology seek to expand our understanding of the universe while the social sciences, humanities, and arts expand our minds to embrace the perspectives of others. Slowly, we awaken to our biases, challenge our faulty norms and improve the collective experience of our species. To the extent that I have the opportunity, I will contribute to this universal mission in my small community of Jehovah's Witnesses.

In the meantime, who else will help the disillusioned JW suffering from RTS as they navigate their trauma? Who will encourage them to overcome their fears and seek professional medical help? Who else can help them recognize that leaving WTS is not indicative of spiritual weakness? Who will make them feel safe while they figure out how to avoid permanent ostracism by their loved ones? Who else will hold the confidence of the freethinking JW who privately chooses lifesaving medical treatment over religious dogma? Who else will use minority influence to moderate a radical community? Who else, but the PIMO?

No doubt, some will interpret my approach as one of silence in the face of oppression and injustice. There is also the danger that future compromises to my individuality for the sake of the JW community will stifle my unique creative potential. Where are these lines in the sand? How do I balance my psychological needs with my desire to affect positive change among Jehovah's Witnesses and bring an end to captive policies and the religious oppression of PIMOs?

These are the questions that lit a delicate wick in my spirit when I was in the depths of Religious Trauma Syndrome's darkness. I felt the first spark of a transcendent spiritual power igniting inside me, and I quickly cupped my hands around the vulnerable little flame. It flickered in the face of fear and uncertainty. But it burned quietly and persistently. Despite my ongoing religious captivity, that little flame of hope lights a path towards liberty that I follow to this day.

> 1/16/19
>
> I woke up today with so much emotional discomfort. Self-honesty can be so constructive, but it is extremely uncomfortable. I feel lost, sad, scared, trapped, and weak. But somewhere inside me, I know that I am finding glorious purpose. Suddenly, I am absorbent of sadness, skillful at undoing anxiety, and freer than I've ever been. And I am powerfully determined to share this state with others.
>
> For now, I have a shining sense of individual purpose. It's beginning to dawn on me that my position as a critical insider is incredibly unique; almost God-assigned (if I were still a believer). I feel a haunting temptation to grasp at an unprecedented spiritual transcendence that lays right before me. It's frightening. But it's the greatness that I always dreamed of.

An Open Letter to the Governing Body

Dear Brothers,

Perhaps you are uncomfortable with me addressing you as my Brothers. But we are all connected as spiritual brothers and sisters in a way that extends beyond the unity of belief. Our spiritual kinship transcends the Christian Congregation of Jehovah's Witnesses, transcends the Holy Scriptures, transcends Jehovah.

My words may sting like a locust strike (Revelation 9:5), but the fact that I have not held back from publishing the criticisms in this volume is evidence of my continued belief in the potential of your human kindness and courage. I am confident that you will identify within yourselves the kind of bravery that will empower you to attain new heights of leadership strength; strength to humbly accept our organization's errors and boldly act to correct the doctrine and policies of Jehovah's Witnesses that "extinguish the smoldering flaxen wick" (Matthew 12:20).

In this context, the "smoldering flaxen wick" is the lowly PIMO; the baptized Jehovah's Witness who can no longer maintain belief in the religious values that they once held so dear. They have supplicated Jehovah to help them maintain their faith in the Watch Tower Bible & Tract Society, but their prayers were not answered in the way they expected. Instead, their magnificent brains drew data from the awe-inspiring creation around them and birthed a new system of beliefs that more adequately addresses their unique spiritual needs. Despite ethical objections to their old system of beliefs, they are unwilling to surrender their loving social and familial relationships by formally disassociating. They remain imprisoned by the policies of our organization.

As you no doubt agree, science is not at odds with true spirituality. This includes the scientific field of psychology. A study of the natural world, human behavior included, can surely be interpreted as peering into the book of creation (Romans 1:20). May the description of my experience with Religious Trauma Syndrome, and the research presented in *A Voice from Inside*, represent just that: evidence from the "book of creation." Evidence that something needs to change. You alone, have the power to make such a change happen by ending the captive policies of disfellowshipping, disassociation, and enforced shunning.

The chariot is on the move (Ezekiel 1:21).

Catch up!

Your Brother,

Geoffrey R. Wallis

Author Bio

Geoffrey Wallis is an active Jehovah's Witness who holds the position of congregation elder in the community. As a critical insider, Wallis uses his unique situation to provide commentary on the social psychology of the organization and raise awareness of how coercion in the group leads to Religious Trauma Syndrome in disillusioned members.

As Wallis puts it in *A Voice from Inside*, he was "heavily involved in both attending and instructing specialized schools and training programs sponsored by the Watch Tower Society." Upon disillusionment, he suffered some of the worst symptoms of religious trauma PTSD including depression, anxiety, panic attacks, and suicidal ideation. Now in full recovery, Wallis puts his family and community relationships in jeopardy to bring awareness to those suffering from religious trauma, and to the challenges of "physically in, mentally out" (PIMO) Jehovah's Witnesses who feel trapped by the policies of the organization.

References

American Psychiatric Association (2013). *Diagnostic and Statistical Manual of Mental Disorders* (5th ed.). https://doi.org/10.1176/appi. books.9780890425596.

Beckford, J.A. (1975). *The Trumpet of Prophecy: A Sociological Study of Jehovah's Witnesses.* Oxford: Blackwell.

Barnes, Haleigh A., Hurley, Robin A., & Taber, Katherine H. (2019) Moral injury and PTSD: Often co-occurring yet mechanistically different. *Journal of Neuropsychiatry and Clinical Neurosciences*, 31(2), A4–103.

Benham, G. (2006). The highly sensitive person: Stress and physical symptom reports. *Personality and Individual Differences*, 40(7), 1433–1440.

Boccia, M., D'Amico, S., Bianchini, F., Marano, A., Giannini, A., Piccardi, L., & Giannini, A.M. (2016). Different neural modifications underpin PTSD after different traumatic events: An fMRI meta-analytic study. *Brain Imaging & Behavior*, 10(1), 226–237. https://doi-org.ezproxy. umgc.edu/10.1007/s11682-015-9387-3.

Chappelle, W., Goodman, T., Reardon, L., & Prince, L. (2019). Combat and operational risk factors for post-traumatic stress disorder symptom criteria among United States air force remotely piloted aircraft "Drone" warfighters. *Journal of Anxiety Disorders*, 62, 86–93. https://doi-org. ezproxy.umgc.edu/10.1016/j.janxdis.2019.01.003.

Chomsky, N. (2015). *What kind of creatures are we?*. Columbia University Press.

Chryssides, G.D. (2016). *Jehovah's Witnesses: Continuity and Change*. London: Routledge.

Csikszentmihalyi, M. (1993). *The Evolving Self: A Psychology for the Third Millennium*. New York: Harper Collins.

Dawkins, R. (2006). *The God Delusion*. Boston: Houghton Mifflin Company.

Franz, R. (1983). Crisis of Conscience (vol. 11). Atlanta, GA: Commentary Press.

Goffman, E. (1963). *Stigma: Notes on the management of spoiled identity*. Simon and Schuster.

Harari, Y.N. (2016). *Sapiens*. Bazarforlag AS.

Herman, J. (2015). *Trauma and Recovery: The Aftermath of Violence— From Domestic Abuse to Political Terror*. New York: Basic Books.

Jonsson, C.O. (1983). The Gentile Times Reconsidered. Atlanta, GA: Contemporary Press.

Jung, C. (1966). The Practice of Psychotherapy (2nd ed.) Princeton, NJ: Princeton University Press.

Kim, S. (2019). Opposition to Motion to Quash. United States District Court for the Northern District of California. Case 3:19-mc-80005-SK. Document 18. https://www.courtlistener.com/docket/8509534/18/in-re-dmca-subpoena-to-reddit-inc/.

Lalich, J., & McLaren, K. (2010). Inside and outcast: Multifaceted stigma and redemption in the lives of gay and lesbian Jehovah's Witnesses. *Journal of Homosexuality, 57*(10), 1303–1333.

Lifton, R.J. (2019). *Losing Reality: On Cults, Cultism, and the Mindset of Political and Religious Zealotry.* New York: The New Press.

Lipka, M. (2016). A closer look at Jehovah's Witnesses living in the U.S. Pew Research Center. https://www.pewresearch.org/fact-tank/2016/04/26/a-closer-look-at-jehovahs-witnesses-living-in-the-u-s/.

Litz, B.T., Stein, N., Delaney, E., Lebowitz, L., Nash, W.P., Silva, C., & Maguen, S. (2009). Moral injury and moral repair in war veterans: A preliminary model and intervention strategy, *Clinical Psychology Review,* 29(8),695–706, ISSN 0272–7358, https://doi.org/10.1016/j.cpr.2009.07.003.

Macmillan, A.H. (1957). *Faith on the March.* New Jersey: Prentice-Hall, Inc.

Maslow, A.H. (1943). A theory of human motivation. *Psychological Review*, 50(4), 370.

Muramoto, O. (1998). Bioethics of the refusal of blood by Jehovah's Witnesses: Part 1. Should bioethical deliberation consider dissidents' views?. *Journal of Medical Ethics*, 24(4), 223–230.

Moscovici, S. (1985). Innovation and minority influence. In S. Moscovici, G. Mugny, & E. van Avermaet (eds), *Perspectives on Minority Influence*, pp. 9–52. Cambridge: Cambridge University Press.

Panchuk, M. (2018). The shattered spiritual self: A philosophical exploration of religious trauma. *Res Philosophica*, 95(3), 505–530.

Quenqua, D. (2019, April 5). A Secret Database of Child Abuse—A former Jehovah's Witness is using stolen documents to expose allegations that the religion has kept hidden for decades. *The Atlantic*.

Religious Order of Jehovah's Witnesses (2015). Application to become a member of the worldwide order of special full-time servants of Jehovah's witnesses. A-8-E. https://avoidjw.org/php/doc/a.php?doc=A-8-E_2015.pdf

Royal Commission into Institutional Responses to Child Sexual Abuse (2015). *Case Study 29: Jehovah's Witnesses.* https://www.childabuseroyalcommission.gov.au/case-studies/case-study-29-jehovahs-witnesses.

Russell, B. (1917). *Political Ideals.* New York: The Century Co.

Sagan, C. (2011). *The Demon-Haunted World: Science as a Candle in the Dark.* New York: Ballantine Books.

Simpson, J.A., & Weiner, E.S.C. (1989). *Oxford English Dictionary.* Oxford: Oxford University Press.

Sun, D., Phillips, R., Mulready, H., Zablonski, S., Turner, J., Turner, M., McClymon, K., Nieuwsma, J., Morey, R. (2019) Resting-state brain fluctuation and functional connectivity dissociate moral injury from posttraumatic stress disorder. *Depression and anxiety, 36*(5), 442–452.

US Supreme Court (1940) *Minersville School District v. Gobitis.*

Watch Tower Bible & Tract Society of Pennsylvania (1938). Organization. The Watchtower, Watchtower Bible & Tract Society of New York, Inc. Brooklyn, New York, p. 182.

Watch Tower Bible & Tract Society of Pennsylvania (1958). Avoid rebellious tendencies. The Watchtower, Watchtower Bible & Tract Society of New York, Inc. Brooklyn, New York, April 1st, p. 219.

Watch Tower Bible & Tract Society of Pennsylvania (1976). Yearbook of Jehovah's Witnesses. Brooklyn, New York: Watchtower Bible & Tract Society of New York, Inc.

Watch Tower Bible & Tract Society of Pennsylvania (1981). Attacking major depression—Professional treatments. The Watchtower, Watchtower Bible & Tract Society of New York, Inc. Brooklyn, New York, October 22nd, p.25.

Watch Tower Bible & Tract Society of Pennsylvania (1987). "A Time to Speak"—When?. Brooklyn, New York: Watchtower Bible & Tract Society of New York, Inc. https://wol.jw.org/en/wol/d/r1/lp-e/1987644.

Watch Tower Bible & Tract Society of Pennsylvania (1992). The real purpose of life. The Watchtower, Watchtower Bible & Tract Society of New York, Inc. Brooklyn, New York, April, p. 8.

Watch Tower Bible & Tract Society of Pennsylvania (1998). Strengthening our faith in God's word. The Watchtower, Watchtower Bible & Tract Society of New York, Inc. Brooklyn, New York, January 15th, p. 26.

Watch Tower Bible & Tract Society of Pennsylvania (2001). Do not let doubts destroy your faith. The Watchtower, Watchtower Bible & Tract Society of New York, Inc. Brooklyn, New York, July 1st, p. 19.

Watch Tower Bible & Tract Society of Pennsylvania (2006). Focus on the goodness of Jehovah's organization. The Watchtower, Watchtower Bible & Tract Society of New York, Inc. Brooklyn, New York, July 15th, p. 22.

Watch Tower Bible & Tract Society of Pennsylvania (2009). Jehovah's wisdom observed in Creation. The Watchtower, Watchtower Bible & Tract Society of New York, Inc. Brooklyn, New York, April 15th, p. 19.

Watch Tower Bible & Tract Society of Pennsylvania (2010). Jehovah's way of ruling vindicated! The Watchtower, Watchtower Bible & Tract Society of New York, Inc. Brooklyn, New York, January 15th, p. 32.

Watch Tower Bible & Tract Society of Pennsylvania (2011a). Do you hate lawlessness?. The Watchtower, Watchtower Bible & Tract Society of New York, Inc. Brooklyn, New York, February 15th, p. 32.

Watch Tower Bible & Tract Society of Pennsylvania (2012a). Questions Young People Ask—Answers That Work, Volume 2. Brooklyn, New York: Watchtower Bible & Tract Society of New York, Inc. https://wol.jw.org/ en/wol/d/r1/lp-e/1102008150.

Watch Tower Bible & Tract Society of Pennsylvania (2012b) Shepherd the Flock of God. Brooklyn, New York: Watchtower Bible & Tract Society of New York, Inc.

Watch Tower Bible & Tract Society of Pennsylvania (2012c) "I am with you" The Watchtower, Watchtower Bible & Tract Society of New York, inc. Brooklyn, New York, August 15th, p.6

Watch Tower Bible & Tract Society of Pennsylvania (2013a). New World Translation of the Holy Scriptures. Brooklyn, New York: Watchtower Bible & Tract Society of New York, Inc. https://wol.jw.org/en/wol/d/r1/ lp-e/2014682#h=1:0-26:914.

Watch Tower Bible & Tract Society of Pennsylvania (2013b). Safeguard your inheritance by making wise choices. The Watchtower, Watchtower Bible & Tract Society of New York, Inc. Brooklyn, New York, May 15th, p. 29.

Watch Tower Bible & Tract Society of Pennsylvania (2013c). Who really is the faithful and discreet slave?. The Watchtower, Watchtower Bible & Tract Society of New York, Inc. Brooklyn, New York, July 15th, p. 22.

Watch Tower Bible & Tract Society of Pennsylvania (2011b). Will you heed Jehovah's clear warnings?. The Watchtower, Watchtower Bible & Tract Society of New York, Inc. Brooklyn, New York, July 15th, p. 16.

Watch Tower Bible & Tract Society of Pennsylvania (2014a). Keep Yourself in God's Love. Brooklyn, New York: Watchtower Bible & Tract Society of New York, Inc.

Watch Tower Bible & Tract Society of Pennsylvania (2014b). Fully Accomplish Your Ministry. Brooklyn, New York: Watchtower Bible & Tract Society of New York, Inc.

Watch Tower Bible & Tract Society of Pennsylvania (2014c). Parents – Shepherd Your children. The Watchtower, Watchtower Bible & Tract Society of New York, Inc. Brooklyn, New York, September 15th, p. 21.

Watch Tower Bible & Tract Society of Pennsylvania (2017a). Winning the Battle for Your Mind. Brooklyn, New York: Watchtower Bible & Tract Society of New York, Inc.

Watch Tower Bible & Tract Society of Pennsylvania (2017b) Are you taking refuge in Jehovah? The Watchtower, Watchtower Bible & Tract Society of New York, Inc. Brooklyn, New York, November, p. 10.

Watch Tower Bible & Tract Society of Pennsylvania (2017c). The truth brings, "not peace, but a sword". The Watchtower, Watchtower Bible & Tract Society of New York, Inc. Brooklyn, New York, October, p. 13.

Watch Tower Bible & Tract Society of Pennsylvania (2018a). What Gift

Can You Give Jehovah? Brooklyn, New York: Watchtower Bible & Tract Society of New York, Inc. https://wol.jw.org/en/wol/d/r1/lp-e/2018649? q=what+gift+can+we+give+Jehovah&p=par.

Watch Tower Bible & Tract Society of Pennsylvania (2018b). Insight on the Scriptures. Brooklyn, New York: Watchtower Bible & Tract Society of New York, Inc.

Watch Tower Bible & Tract Society of Pennsylvania (2018c). Gerrit Lösch: In whom do you trust? Patterson, New York: Watchtower Bible & Tract Society of New York, Inc. https://www.jw.org/en/library/videos/#en/mediaitems/StudioTalks/pub-jwb_201803_2_VIDEO

Watch Tower Bible & Tract Society of Pennsylvania (2019a). Shepherd the Flock of God. Brooklyn, New York: Watchtower Bible & Tract Society of New York, Inc. https://www.yumpu.com/s/KQ9L34McNkjyH7Wf.

Watch Tower Bible & Tract Society of Pennsylvania (2019b). Organized to Do Jehovah's Will. Brooklyn, New York: Watchtower Bible & Tract Society of New York, Inc.

Watch Tower Bible & Tract Society of Pennsylvania (2020a). Examining the Scriptures Daily. Brooklyn, New York: Watchtower Bible & Tract Society of New York, Inc.

Watch Tower Bible & Tract Society of Pennsylvania (2020b). How to conduct a Bible study that leads to baptism—Part One. The Watchtower, Watchtower Bible & Tract Society of New York, Inc. Brooklyn, New York, October, p. 8.

Watch Tower Bible & Tract Society of Pennsylvania (2020c). The Resurrection reveals God's love, wisdom, and patience. The Watchtower,

Watchtower Bible & Tract Society of New York, Inc. Brooklyn, New York, August, p. 19.

Watch Tower Bible & Tract Society of Pennsylvania (2020d). Do Jehovah's witnesses break up families or build them up? Watchtower Bible & Tract Society of New York, Inc. Brooklyn, New York. https://www.jw.org/en/jehovahs-witnesses/faq/families/

Watch Tower Bible & Tract Society of Pennsylvania. Sing Praises to Jehovah.

Winell, M. (2006). *Leaving the Fold.* Berkeley, CA: Apocryphile Press.

Winell, M. (2011) Religious trauma—Part Three: The trauma of leaving religion. *Cognitive Behaviour Therapy Today*, November.

Zieman, B. (2018). Psychological conflicts of a Jehovah's Witness patient. *Advocates for Jehovah's Witness Reform on Blood.* https://ajwrb.org.

Printed in Great Britain
by Amazon